VEGETABLE PRODUCTION AND VALUE CHAINS IN MONGOLIA

AUGUST 2020

ASIAN DEVELOPMENT BANK

Note:
In this publication, "$" refers to United States dollars.

On the cover: Vegetable market in "Autumn Green Days" expo in Ulaanbaatar (photo by Bold Bolorchimeg).

CONTENTS

TABLES AND FIGURES..v
FOREWORD..vii
ACKNOWLEDGMENTS...viii
ABBREVIATIONS..ix
EXECUTIVE SUMMARY...x

1. KEY FINDINGS...1

1.1 Current Situation and Prospects: Market and Value Chain...1
1.2 Potential Improvement: Models, Feasibility, High-Level Investment Assessment,
    and Business Models for Value Chain Players 1
    1.2.1 Potential Improvements for the Community Grower Groups 2
    1.2.2 Potential Improvements for Traders, Aggregators, and Wholesalers..................................2
    1.2.3 Potential Improvements for Processors and Retailers..3
1.3 Recommendations for Approach to Public–Private Sector Engagement...................................3
    1.3.1 Actionable Recommendations on How to Support Community Grower Groups.......................3
    1.3.2 Identification of Types of Vertical and Horizontal Coordination Models.............................4
    1.3.3 Actions to Facilitate Increased Value Chain Coordination..5

2. MARKET ASSESSMENT.. 6

2.1 Sector Overview... 6
    2.1.1 Introduction 6
    2.1.2 Historical Context..6
    2.1.3 Policy Context 7
2.2 Demand Analysis: Who, Where, Products, Quantities, Qualities, Prices,
    Trends, and Prospects 9
    2.2.1 Demand (Consumption)...9
    2.2.2 Relevance of Food Safety Assurance and Quality Standards... 17
2.3 Supply Analysis.. 20
    2.3.1 Market Size: Where Is Produce Grown, How, and in What Quantity? 20
    2.3.2 Supply Analysis: What Vegetables and Where From?...20
2.4 Drivers of Supply Performance..33

3. VALUE CHAIN ANALYSIS.. 34

3.1 Value Chain Map: Marketing Channels, Revenues, Costs, Margins, and Trends 34
    3.1.1 Description of the End-to-End Value Chain for Vegetables in Mongolia 34
3.2 Competitive Market Landscape: Shares of Domestic Suppliers, Imports,
    Nature of Competition, and Trends.. 38
    3.2.1 Who Are the Major Suppliers of Promising Crops? 38
    3.2.2 Analysis of Product Prices in Ulaanbaatar Markets 41
    3.2.3 Distribution of Margins Across Segments of Relevant Value Chains............................... 41

3.3   Strengths and Weaknesses of Value Chains in Meeting Market Needs for Volume,
       Price, and Quality.. 50
       3.3.1   Discussions of Key Results 50
       3.3.2   Procurement Sources, Producers, and Sources of Raw Materials..................... 52
       3.3.3   Evaluation of Imported Crops and Raw Materials, Prospects of Competition, and
                Scope for Import Substitution 52
       3.3.4   Sources of Critical Inputs and Technologies.. 54
3.4   Role of Smallholder Farmers in Meeting Value Chain Needs 56

4. TECHNICAL ANALYSIS: CONNECTING SMALLHOLDER FARMERS TO MARKETS 57

4.1   Introduction 57
4.2   Models for Potential Improvement of Smallholder Community Grower Groups in
       Project *Soums* to Meet Market Needs.. 57
       4.2.1   Base Case Model... 58
       4.2.2   Alternative Crops Model 59
       4.2.3   Value Chain Models 60
       4.2.4   Key Constraints for Market Entry and Access to High-Value Markets 66
       4.2.5   Actions to Overcome Constraints... 67
       4.2.6   Farm-Level Economic Analysis and Financial Requirements............................. 68
4.3   Analysis of Input Supply, Processing, Marketing, and Distribution 70
       4.3.1   Key Constraints, Actions, and Investments by the Public and
                Private Sectors 71
       4.3.2   Potential Establishment of Contract Arrangements to Facilitate Connecting the
                Community Grower Groups to Markets 71
       4.3.3   Key Constraints for Downstream Value Chain Participants................................ 72
       4.3.4   Feasibility of Improvements: Technical, Commercial, Financial, Social,
                and Scalability 73

5. CONNECTING SMALLHOLDER VEGETABLE FARMERS TO MARKETS
   IN OTHER DEVELOPING CENTRAL ASIAN COUNTRIES 75

5.1   Kazakhstan 75
5.2   Uzbekistan.. 76
5.3   Pakistan 76

6. RECOMMENDED APPROACH FOR PUBLIC SECTOR PROJECTS
   TO INCREASE FARMING INCOMES 77

6.1   Approach to Public Sector Projects.. 77
6.2   Approach to Private Sector Engagement 77
6.3   Recommendations.. 77

APPENDIX... 80

TABLES AND FIGURES

TABLES

1   Apparent Consumption of Vegetables, 2012–2017 10
2   Estimated Vegetable Market Value, 2012–2017 11
3   Production, Markets, and Storage of Local Field and Greenhouse Crops 12
4   Vegetable Production Self-Sufficiency Rate, 2012–2017 13
5   Urban and Rural Population of Mongolia, 2012–2017 14
6   Urban and Rural Per Capita Average Annual Vegetable Consumption, 2012–2016 14
7   Difference between Urban and Rural Per Capita Average Annual Vegetable Consumption, 2012–2016 15
8   Nationwide Consumption of Potato and Vegetables, 2017 15
9   Average Potential Market Size of Vegetables, by Volume..16
10 Estimation of Potential Consumption of Vegetables, 2018–2020 16
11 Valuation of Market Size for Potato and Vegetables in Urban and Rural Areas, by Volume, 2018–2020 17
12 Examples of Food Safety Practices Along the Value Chain 19
13 Vegetable Farm Production, by Volume, 2012–2017 21
14 Potato, Vegetables, Cereals, and Fodder Crop Production, by Harvest Volume, 2012–2017 22
15 Total Yield of Potato and Vegetables, by *Aimag*, 2017...23
16 Vegetable Farm Production Volume in the Project *Soums*, 2014–2016 24
17 Potato and Vegetable Production Volume in the Project *Soums*, Share in the National Total, 2014–2016 24
18 Vegetable Plantation Areas in the Project *Soums*, 2014–2016 25
19 Vegetable Yield in the Project *Soums*, 2014–2016 25
20 Summary of Growing Degree Days of Vegetables Cultivated in the Project *Soums*..........27
21 Planting Start Date and Growth Length of Vegetables Cultivated in the Project *Soums* 28
22 Market Availability of Most and Least Commonly Produced Vegetables in Mongolia 29
23 Summary of Customs Import Data of Vegetables, 2015–2017 30
24 Vegetable Import Volumes, 2012–2017...31
25 Vegetable Import Values, 2012–2017..31
26 Unit Prices of Imported Vegetables, 2012–2017 32
27 Production of Potato and Vegetable Suppliers, 2016...38
28 Smallholder Vegetable Growers' Contributions to Potato and Vegetable Production, 2016..........39
29 Number of Mongolian-Based Companies Involved in Potato and Vegetable Imports, 2017 41
30 Main Value Chains for Potatoes and Vegetables in Mongolia 41
31 Value Chain 1—Farm Gate to Traders and/or Large Suppliers to Wholesalers to Markets and/or Supermarkets 43
32 Value Chain 2—Large and/or Medium-Scale Farmers to Name Stores, Supermarkets, or Other Retail Points to Consumers..45
33 Value Chain 3—Importers to Traders and/or Large Suppliers to Wholesalers to Markets and/or Supermarkets (Retailers) to Consumers..47
34 Value Chain 4—Smallholder Farmers and/or Individual Growers or Importers to Processing Factories to Markets and/or Supermarkets (Retailers) to Consumers 48

35   Value Chain 5—Smallholder Farmers and/or Individual Growers or
      Large and/or Medium-Scale Farmers to Large Retailer "C" to Consumers...................................49
36   Share of Main Value Chains in Total Demand for Retail Sales in Mongolia...52
37   Summary of Vegetables Imported into Mongolia, 2017 53
38   Daily Potato and Vegetable Intake for Standard Population in Urban and Rural Areas...................54
39   Annual Food Demand for Standard Population, 2013–2016...54
40   Value-Added Imported Vegetable Products, 2017 55
41   Number of Proposed Investments Based on Farm Size...59
42   Key Assumptions of the Value Chain Models...62
43   Key Parameters of the Value Chain Models...64
44   Farm-Level Investments under the Alternative Crops Model 67
45   Investments under the Value Chain Models 67
46   Farm-Level Impacts of the Alternative Crops Model 68
47   Income and Returns for All Models 69
48   Key Constraints and Actions Required by the Private and Public Sectors.................................71

FIGURES

1   Average Unit Price of Imported Vegetables versus Currency Exchange Rate, 2012–2017 32
2   Simplified Mapping of Vegetable Value Chain in Mongolia 34
3   Vegetable Value Chain Dynamics in Mongolia...35
4   Structure of Potato and Vegetable Supply Chain, 2016...39
5   Crop Farming Product Use, 2015 40

FOREWORD

Mongolia's economy has been characterized by rapid growth and transformation since transitioning from central planning in the early 1990s. Mineral exports were the main driver for achieving middle-income status in 2011. However, Mongolia's vulnerability to external shocks underscored the need for a more diversified and labor-intensive economic structure for the rural population. Limited income-generating opportunities and lack of resilience to natural disasters increase the risk of rural–urban migration. Agriculture is not sufficiently diversified and relies heavily on livestock production. Only about half of the country's vegetable demand was met by domestic production during 2008–2016.

Vegetables are in high demand by more health-conscious citizens, and a more balanced diet can be expected to have considerable public health benefits. Increased vegetable production will provide the opportunity for increased vegetable consumption, particularly in rural areas, which will have a positive impact on providing essential nutrients, energy, and vitamins to support dietary diversity and a balanced diet for the general population. Benefits to children of an improved diet can be expected to reduce stunting. Vegetable production provides an ideal opportunity for poverty reduction since it is particularly suited to small land areas, intensively uses labor, and matches the resource availability of the poor. In addition, the responsibilities of women in vegetable production contribute to the effective gender mainstreaming classification of the project.

The Asian Development Bank supports the government's focus to accelerate economic diversification and job creation. Agriculture has become a priority for growth. It is the main source of livelihood in rural areas, where more than one-third of the total population lives and poverty remains higher than in urban areas.

In close cooperation with the Government of Mongolia's Ministry of Food, Agriculture and Light Industry, this knowledge product was prepared to provide information and analyses of selected aspects of smallholder vegetable production and market access for improved self-sufficiency and reduced rural poverty. This publication aims to move the country's agricultural diversification policy agenda forward and attract donor support for climate-resilient vegetable production activities.

James Lynch
Director General
East Asia Department
Asian Development Bank

ACKNOWLEDGMENTS

This publication is based on the findings of a study under the regional technical assistance (TA) project of the Asian Development Bank, TA 9057-REG: Building Sustainable Food and Nutrition Security in Asia and the Pacific, led by Jan F. Hinrichs and with technical review by Michiko Katagami.

The technical study report was prepared by the TA consultants Charlotte Bisley, Tserenkhan Gurbadam, Selwyn Heilbron, Altanbadralt Sharkhuu, and Shinee Volooj. Their consulting work comprised a combination of desk research, field visits, and surveys undertaken from March to June 2018 in Ulaanbaatar and selected *soums* (districts) of four of Mongolia's *aimags* (provinces): Bornuur in Tuv, Orkhon in Darkhan-Uul, Ulaangom in Uvs, and Yeruu in Selenge.

We appreciate the invaluable information provided by the government agencies, enterprises, farmers' cooperatives, family farms, and farmers who graciously accommodated the TA consultants' field visits and surveys.

ABBREVIATIONS

ADB	Asian Development Bank
CAGR	compound annual growth rate
CGG	community grower group
CO_2	carbon dioxide
GDD	growing degree day
LDT	lower development threshold
LLC	Limited Liability Company
MFARD	Mongolian Farmer Association for Rural Development
MNT	Mongolian togrog
MOFALI	Ministry of Food, Agriculture and Light Industry
NGO	nongovernment organization
NPV	net present value
NSO	National Statistical Office
PSARI	Plant Science and Agricultural Research Institute
SDC	Swiss Agency for Development and Cooperation
VEGI	Inclusive and Sustainable Vegetable Production and Marketing Project

WEIGHTS AND MEASURES

g	gram
ha	hectare
kg	kilogram
kt	kiloton
m^2	square meter

EXECUTIVE SUMMARY

The agriculture sector plays a significant role in the Mongolian economy, both in revenue generation and employment. Within that sector, vegetable production (with 17,415 small-scale and part-time smallholder growers) is an important contributor to economic, social, and nutritional outcomes.

This report analyzes the market for vegetables and the value chain for vegetable products as they move from producers to consumers. It focuses on four target *soums* (districts)—Bornuur in Tuv, Orkhon in Darkhan-Uul, Ulaangom in Uvs, and Yeruu in Selenge—that together account for around 14% of national production. The strategy of the Asian Development Bank (ADB) for the agriculture sector aims at diversifying the economy to increase income-generating and employment opportunities in rural areas. The market analysis focuses on smallholder vegetable production to maximize the employment and rural income impact of ADB's projects. Smallholder vegetable production is predominant, and the underlying study was a preparation for further ADB lending support to the sector. Vegetable production provides an ideal opportunity for poverty reduction since it is particularly suited to small land areas, intensively uses labor, and matches the resource availability of the poor. Limited income-generating opportunities and lack of resilience to natural disasters increase the risk for rural–urban migration. Diversification of the agriculture sector has lagged behind with a high reliance on imports for vegetables and fodder, which in turn threatens national food security. Food insecurity is also higher in rural areas. For example, the prevalence of underweight children under 5 years old is 2.2% in rural areas (including *soum* centers) and 1.2% in urban areas, while the prevalence of stunting (height for age) is 20.3% in rural areas compared to 12.7% in urban areas. Vegetables are in high demand by more health-conscious citizens, and a more balanced diet can be expected to have considerable public health benefits. Increased vegetable production will provide the opportunity for increased vegetable consumption, particularly in rural areas, which will have a positive impact on providing essential nutrients, energy, and vitamins to support dietary diversity and a balanced diet for the general population. Benefits to children of an improved diet are expected to be substantial, including reduction in the high rates of stunting.

Mongolia is a net importer of vegetables, and government policy favors import substitution. Mongolia is self-sufficient in meat, which is a significant export, and potatoes. However, it produces only about two-thirds of its needs for other vegetables, which are imported during the off-season at higher prices, representing an opportunity for income substitution and economic gain. After the collapse of the Soviet Union, government support for national and regional crop research and extension centers declined. Cultivation techniques are unsustainable for water productivity, and the impacts of climate change have led to increased droughts. Productivity is further limited by lack of access to high-yield and climate-resilient varieties of seeds. Mongolia currently imports about $114.00 million worth of vegetables and other unprocessed food products including, for example, $5.15 million in cabbages and $3.62 million in onions. Consumption has been fairly stagnant since 2015 and is falling below levels recommended by national nutritional guidelines.

The value chain for vegetables features multiple transactions with intermediaries adding significant costs. Farmers struggle to generate returns that would justify capital investments in irrigation, mechanization, and greenhouses that would lengthen the growing season and enable increased yields.

Most smallholder farmers choose to sell products to traders and intermediaries because traders arrive at farms in their own vehicles and purchase vegetables in exchange for cash at farm gate prices. Lacking storage facilities, farmers generally sell all their produce at once, close to harvest time when prices are weakest.

Bypassing such intermediaries by selling directly to retailers and institutional buyers would potentially generate higher prices for farmers. However, not all farmers can meet the quality specifications set by retailers in response to consumer demands.

Moreover, retailers generally do not pay at the time of purchase, and may apply a "wastage" deduction for produce that is spoiled in transit or cannot be sold. Furthermore, smallholder farmers typically lack sufficient marketing skills to add value to their products.

This report identifies the costs and returns, as well as required capital investment, of improving vegetable production with and without changes to the value chain. It explores the potential for farmers to sell directly to farm stalls, vegetable processors, retailers, or a centralized wholesale center. It contains practical recommendations for implementing these approaches.

Women in Mongolia play a significant role in smallholder vegetable production and value addition. A recent gender assessment conducted by the Swiss Agency for Development and Cooperation found that while fewer women held managerial positions, there were more female than male farmers at the producer level and in agricultural extension centers. Typically, however, vegetable farming is a family business in which all the members participate.

Government support and advocacy for greenhouses in recent years has enabled women's involvement in production of vegetables with a higher marginal value such as leafy greens, as these can be grown in greenhouses close to their homes.

1 KEY FINDINGS

1.1 Current Situation and Prospects: Market and Value Chain

Below is a current high-level summary of key insights and findings of the work:

- Statistics indicate that the volume of vegetable imports is growing. This suggests strong underlying demand for some vegetables.

- Mongolia is self-sufficient in potatoes, but produces only about two-thirds of its needs for other vegetables. Self-sufficiency is especially low in relatively higher-value vegetables such as garlic.

- Based on the 2017 data from the National Statistical Office (NSO) of Mongolia, the annual per capita consumption rates were about 111.3 grams (g)/day for potatoes and 142.4 g/day for vegetables, which is less than the 120 g/day of potatoes and 260 g/day of vegetables recommended by the Ministry of Health.[1] While current potato production almost meets the per capita recommendation, vegetable production needs to be increased by around 45%.

- Farmers sell vegetables along complex value chains. The largest price margins, or "spreads," between the prices for purchase and sale of vegetables along these chains are captured by wholesalers and traders. Processors add significantly to prices, but also have significant costs. This indicates the importance of considering both the profit and price margins.

- Preliminary indications suggest that farming vegetables produces a negligible return (measured in terms of cash profit relative to sales revenue) for smallholder farmers, but a reasonable return for most medium-sized farms. Profit margins for processing and retailing appear unremarkable.

1.2 Potential Improvement: Models, Feasibility, High-Level Investment Assessment, and Business Models for Value Chain Players

Key opportunities to improve value chains are discussed below:

- In addition to alternative crops and production methods, farmers could increase the prices they receive through changes in the value chains that they use. In theory, more direct routes to market offer the opportunity to reduce the value captured by intermediaries and give farmers a higher share of the total value generated along the chain to consumers.

---

[1] Government of Mongolia, Ministry of Health. 2017. *Decree No. A/74*. Ulaanbaatar. 23 February.

- There are significant opportunities for farmers to enhance value chain outcomes and secure higher prices through direct relationships with processors and retailers. However, farmers must be able to meet the requirements of their customers for volume, quality, and delivery.

- There are also opportunities for farmers to increase returns from improved wholesale selling conditions. This entails the development of new storage, transport, and selling facilities, and regulation of competition.

- Given the need for increased supply volumes and the small size of current farm operations, community grower groups (CGGs) could be established to improve coordination and delivery of investment in goods and services, such as capacity building and knowledge products.

These developments, taken together, should enable the current volume of imports to be replaced with domestic production in the near term. This will require support and investment from other private sector participants, the Government of Mongolia, and the Asian Development Bank (ADB).

Production of seeds in Mongolia, tailored to its growing conditions, should be expanded through the provision of additional infrastructure for seed multiplication by research institutes, in collaboration with private seed companies.

1.2.1 Potential Improvements for the Community Grower Groups

The following are potential improvements specific to CGGs.

- CGGs should develop group brands, especially for high-value vegetables, in close collaboration with retailers, including through co-branding.

- CGGs should evaluate, with their retail partners, the development of group packaging and labeling of produce that meets consumer needs. Where economically justified and supported by strategic marketing relationships, support should be given to CGGs' purchase of packaging and labeling facilities.

- A year-round increase in supply can be facilitated by expanding the number of greenhouses, especially winter greenhouses. This could be supported by an approach similar to ADB's Agriculture and Rural Development Project on financial intermediaries for enabling the expansion of processing facilities. Particular attention should be given to training farmers in production technology through CGGs and learning from the experience of successful greenhouse producers.

1.2.2 Potential Improvements for Traders, Aggregators, and Wholesalers

The main aim of the improvements identified in this project is to increase the incomes of vegetable farmers. However, improvements in the alternative crops model would increase the quantity and quality of vegetables available throughout the value chain and, hence, would better meet customer demand. These benefits would accrue to traders, aggregators, and wholesalers commensurate with their ability to meet those customer demands.

The market environment in which traders, aggregators, and wholesalers strive to meet those needs will, however, change. The value chain improvements identified in this report envisage that farmers will be able to sell more produce directly to consumers, processors, and retailers by increasing the volume, quality, and continuity of supply. This will place additional competitive pressure on intermediaries to provide value for the services they provide.

Under the alternative crops model, shared storage facilities in rural areas under CGGs' control will increase farmers' bargaining power with traders and aggregators. In addition, the availability of significant storage and sales facilities at wholesale centers will increase farmers' bargaining power with retailers, in competition with other wholesalers.

1.2.3 Potential Improvements for Processors and Retailers

Processors and retailers will be able to rely on an increased volume, quality, and continuity of vegetable supplies. This will reduce the risk of investment and improve returns. To the extent that this reduces the need for vegetable imports, it will also reduce the risks associated with foreign exchange transactions.

1.3 Recommendations for Approach to Public–Private Sector Engagement

Below are some key recommendations for public and private sector engagement in the context of ADB's current and planned initiatives for the agriculture sector:

- The adequacy of the current competition regulation relating to farm produce supply should be reviewed, and the potential for introducing codes of conduct and standard form contracts for produce sales by farmers should be examined. This will strengthen the farmers' bargaining power in their direct dealings with processors and retailers.

- The statistical basis for vegetable pricing, including those along the supply chain, needs to be enhanced to cover production of vegetables currently in demand, such as green leafy vegetables, and be consistent with statistics on imports of these products.

1.3.1 Actionable Recommendations on How to Support Community Grower Groups

Specific recommendations on how to support CGGs and other market players within ADB's Community Vegetable Farming for Livelihood Improvement Project are discussed below:

- Development of farm stalls where vegetable producers, especially smallholder producers, can eliminate intermediary costs and sell directly to consumers and should be piloted at selected points in Ulaanbaatar and in relatively high-traffic rural locations, e.g., near auto and railroad crossings. The trials should assess the economic cost–benefit for farmers of selling via this value chain.

■ By directly supplying vegetables to processors, farmers can eliminate intermediary costs and potentially increase their returns. Increased vegetable processing would encourage more use of this value chain. This can be facilitated through additional large-scale processing investments similar to ADB's Agriculture and Rural Development Project on financial intermediaries. These facilities could be located in production supply areas within target *soums* (i.e., Bornuur in Tuv, Orkhon in Darkhan-Uul, Ulaangom in Uvs, and Yeruu in Selenge), if economically feasible, or in Ulaanbaatar. Processors should be encouraged to implement supply contracts with CGGs in the target *soums* (see also the recommendation relating to fair trading legislation).

■ Supplying vegetables directly to retailers can also eliminate intermediary costs and potentially increase farmers' returns. Retailers should be encouraged to enter into strategic partnership arrangements with CGGs to support year-round supply of produce that meets retailer standards.

1.3.2   Identification of Types of Vertical and Horizontal Coordination Models

In terms of vertical arrangements, there is considerable potential to establish contract arrangements between farmers and processors, and between farmers and retailers. This would reduce transaction costs and improve returns to farmers and retailers, while meeting consumer needs. The establishment of wholesale centers would also facilitate direct sales between farmers and wholesalers, and between farmers and retailers.

The application of network-connected information technology along the entire value chain from production to marketing would reduce contract arrangement and monitoring costs between farmers and retailers through traceability and market information with a two-way automated information exchange system. It would provide consumers with food safety-related product information, while producers get access to market information.

The success of this arrangement would be dependent on economic conditions. Farmers must be able to supply the volumes of produce required on time and meet quality requirements, including food safety. A competition framework that facilitates a balance of bargaining power between concerned parties is also necessary.

In terms of horizontal arrangements, CGGs should facilitate training and knowledge-sharing between farmers, promote economies of scale in supply through joint ownership of assets and/or marketing of produce (including development of farmer-owned brands), and increase farmers' bargaining power in vertical arrangements.

It is suggested that the CGGs be modelled on the Greenhouse Vegetable Growers Federation and similar groups. Such groups could form the umbrella organizations to support the management of CGGs and cooperatives. The CGGs could own common assets such as greenhouses and storage facilities, where appropriate, and lease those assets to individual farmers. The CGGs would need to have appropriate legal status enabling them to conduct commercial activities along with commensurate formal governance arrangements. Training and infrastructure support (such as appropriate office facilities) as well as support for legislative or regulatory changes would be required for the establishment of the CGGs.

1.3.3 Actions to Facilitate Increased Value Chain Coordination

The major infrastructure, business, and investment actions required of downstream public and private participants are summarized as follows:

Public sector. Financing of alternative crops model investment, construction of farm stalls for the stalls value chain model, financing of a new facility in the processing value chain model, and feasibility and construction of a wholesale center. Training and infrastructure support for CGGs would be required, as would a review of competition regulation and establishment of an enabling competition environment.

Private sector. Undertaking asset investments in all models, except for a wholesale selling center.

2 MARKET ASSESSMENT

2.1 Sector Overview

2.1.1 Introduction

The agriculture sector plays a significant role in the Mongolian economy, in both revenue generation and employment. For instance, in 2016, the agriculture sector generated about 13% of the country's gross domestic product and directly or indirectly employed more than half of its 3 million people.

According to the Bank of Mongolia, the country spends around $500 million on food imports annually.[2] However, the Mongolian vegetable industry has been transitioning to replace imported vegetables. A recent World Bank-supported agricultural productivity and marketing study implies that Mongolia produces roughly 60% of its own vegetable consumption.[3] This raises important issues related to national food security and highlights good prospects and opportunities for local smallholder farmers and growers.

2.1.2 Historical Context

Private vegetable farming is a relatively new industry in Mongolia. Historically and culturally, the main diet of nomadic and pastoralist Mongolians did not include many vegetables. The main staples were meat, dairy, flour, and naturally grown herbs and fruits. Vegetable farming and, hence, consumption on a wider scale only increased after the state collective farming movement during the socialist era in the 1950s. As a result, some common vegetables such as potato, onion, carrots, and cabbage slowly became part of Mongolia's staple diet.

During the socialist regime, collective farms were responsible for crop and vegetable production at national and local levels, and the centralized supply and distribution system took charge of marketing and logistics. Before the 2000s, almost all large-scale state collective vegetable farms operating in the cropping region were dismantled and privatized. This led to the deterioration of farm infrastructure and facilities as they were left without maintenance and safeguarding. The collapse of these collective farms compelled many rural Mongolians who were formerly employed by them to commence subsistence-scale vegetable production. The dismantling of the collective farms left many rural households without clear direction about their rights to use cropland and how to start their household farming initiatives.

---

[2] United States Department of Commerce International Trade Administration. 2016. *Mongolia Country Commercial Guide 2016*. https://photos.state.gov/libraries/mongolia/5/business/2016-Country-Commercial-Guide.pdf

[3] D.L. Rasmussen and C. Annor-Frempong. 2015. *Agricultural Productivity and Marketing*. Washington, DC: World Bank.

2.1.3 Policy Context

The Government of Mongolia provided support to the vegetable sector between 1997 and 2012 through the Green Revolution National Programme. With the inception of the National Programme on Vegetables in 2017, support to the sector resumed and is scheduled to run until 2022. The program aims to support a sustainable annual supply of domestically produced vegetables by promoting initiatives for small-scale household farms, smallholder farmers, and cooperatives focused on diversification and production of vegetables. The National Programme on Vegetables has four major components, initially to be implemented during 2018–2020:

- Support diversification of vegetables and increase the efficient production of each scalable land area to supply people with fresh vegetables even during winter and spring seasons and decrease reliance on imported vegetables.

- Introduce state-of-the-art technology to intensify vegetable farm production and irrigation systems, reward investments that increase storage capacity, and develop and support direct marketplaces for vegetables.

- Support seed production, and test additional healthy and productive seeds to increase both quality and supply.

- Enhance the knowledge and skills of vegetable farmers and hire qualified specialists to improve industrial human resources.

In 2008, the government approved the Atar 3 Campaign National Programme under the National Development Action Plan for 2008–2012.[4] The campaign aimed to improve food security and safety by (i) improving the legal and economic environment for crop production, and (ii) increasing domestic production of safe and locally produced crops and vegetables. Major targets were directed to cultivate abandoned crop fields, improve access to and availability of quality vegetable seeds, and transfer advanced technology for vegetable production. The campaign was considered by agriculturalists to be a rescue action for recovery of the crop farming sector, which had been in decline since the 1990s due to the dismantling and privatization of the large-scale state collective vegetable farms.

According to the 2012 end-of-programme assessment of the Ministry of Food, Agriculture and Light Industry (MOFALI), implementation of the campaign resulted in supply to the domestic market of 78% of wheat, 100% of potatoes, 54% of vegetables, and 5% of fruits.

The Atar 3 Campaign National Programme has continued under consecutive government national development plans and is still being implemented; the current phase runs up to 2020. Its focus is advanced technology transfer, such as water retention and soil protection technologies, as well as development of the vegetable seed production industry. The current phase aims to achieve self-sufficiency in wheat and commonly consumed vegetables (e.g., potato, carrot, cabbage, turnip, onion) and 50% sufficiency in fodder plants production for cattle farming.

---

[4]   The word "atar" means virgin land. During socialist times, the Government of Mongolia implemented two campaigns for cultivating virgin land in the cropping regions, which resulted in the development of the crop production industry in Mongolia. The volume of cultivated land under these two campaigns reached 1.5 million hectares.

Through the Atar 3 Campaign National Programme, the government has supported the development of AgroPark Extension centers in each *soum*, which has increased local capacity for specialty vegetable production. In addition, each *soum* has obtained a direct input of MNT2.5 million worth of cold-frame greenhouses, MNT5.0 million to construct underground storage, and one small-scale tractor.

Although the Atar 3 Campaign National Programme has improved domestic production and decreased the volume of imports, the total market demand for vegetables with high nutritional value has not been fully met.

The Atar 3 Campaign National Programme has been able to target domestic wheat producers and provide necessary financial support to improve the technology and seed reserve base. Wheat producers credit the program with improving self-sufficiency and increasing the domestically produced wheat seed reserve base. Domestic mill companies are no longer reliant on imported wheat to cover consumers' needs for wheat flour, and this has contributed to the sustainability of wheat and flour products. It has also contributed significantly to Mongolia's food security, as these are staple food items.

The government's focus on increased crop production was also evidenced through Parliamentary Decree No.12 of 2008. Its Strategic Goal 2 was "to improve land usage, develop irrigation farming and biotechnology to increase crop production", while Strategic Goal 6 called for "the introduction of advanced technologies aimed at protecting the soil from erosion, maintaining fertility, and reducing moisture evaporation." Similarly, the Agriculture Sector Development Policy, 2016–2021 aims to support the agriculture sector over the long term by reducing risk in agricultural production and ensuring sustainable development. Key strategies to achieve this have been identified as supporting greenhouse production; improving production of berries and fruits, and specialty vegetables; increasing irrigation farming; and establishing warehousing and logistics centers in agricultural regions. The policy also aims to increase the export of agricultural products, like high-quality sea buckthorn, by introducing product testing. Mongolian medicinal plants have been identified as a sector with significant export potential.

The Law on Cropland, 2004 (revised 2016) provides the regulatory framework for cropland soil protection and rejuvenation measures. According to this law, farmers and farming enterprises are required to provide soil samples every 5 years for analysis by a certified soil laboratory. Local *soum* and *aimag* (province) government administrations, which are responsible for inspections and control over cropland soil conditions and soil pollution, require these analytical reports to extend land lease contracts or grant land-use permissions.

Cropland soil testing is required for any type of land-use practices, changes in type of crops, and introduction of technological innovations. Few certified laboratories are authorized to implement soil testing for nutrient availability and provide testing services for farmers. The existing authorized soil laboratories are located at the Geo-Ecology Institute, the Mongolian University of Life Science, and the Plant Science and Agricultural Research Institute (PSARI).

At the National Seminar on Soil Laboratory Methods and Analysis held on 10–11 May 2018 at PSARI, major recommendations were presented to address challenges associated with soil testing information coordination and exchange, unified sampling and testing methods, and database development.

Large-scale producers normally use the services of certified laboratories, but vegetable growers and buyers do not have adequate knowledge on soil quality and pollution. During a focus group discussion, farmers in Bornuur stated that soil testing results and certifications are not required when their produce are sold to wholesalers in major markets in Ulaanbaatar.

The Law on Organic Food is seen by MOFALI as facilitating a legal environment for shaping comprehensive plant protection measures, protecting cropland from soil degradation and erosion, improving productivity of soil, and phasing in balanced rotation of plant cultures and zero tillage technology.[5]

These policy priorities acknowledge that meeting the vegetable demands of heavily populated cities and *aimags* through household farming presents a major challenge. There is, therefore, a significant focus on intensifying agricultural production and harvesting by upgrading technical equipment and providing soft loans to support technological advancement. There is also a focus on establishing equipment maintenance centers in agricultural regions.

The government has provided particular support for potatoes and other vegetables. It has imposed tariffs on imported fruits and vegetables linked to relevant years' harvests and implemented flexible pricing for imported goods. It has also increased the number of open market kiosks in Ulaanbaatar and *aimags* to support domestic vegetable procurement.

2.2 Demand Analysis: Who, Where, Products, Quantities, Qualities, Prices, Trends, and Prospects

This section of the report summarizes the demand analysis undertaken by the consulting team.

2.2.1 Demand (Consumption)

Total vegetable consumption figures have been calculated using the following formula:

Total consumption (*demand*) = [Farm production (*local supply*) + Imports (*external supply*)] – Exports

Table 1 summarizes estimated consumption of vegetables in Mongolia during 2012–2017. With the exception of onions and garlic, both vegetable farm production and import volumes decreased during this period, which led to a reduction in the total consumption of vegetables, as illustrated by the calculated compound annual growth rate (CAGR) of –9%.

---

5   Government of Mongolia, MOFALI. 2018. *The Food, Agriculture and Light Industry Sector Gender-Responsive Policy, 2018–2025.* Ulaanbaatar.

Table 1: Apparent Consumption of Vegetables, 2012–2017
('000 ton)

Item	2012	2013	2014	2015	2016	2017	CAGR (%)
Potato	249.1	189.1	162.4	180.9	166.0	121.6	(13)
Vegetables, specified	168.5	161.5	165.0	117.6	151.3	134.7	(4)
Cabbage	54.7	43.7	42.6	39.9	41.3	45.2	(4)
Carrot, turnip	75.1	67.3	67.7	37.7	57.0	43.7	(10)
Onion, garlic	16.0	25.5	28.5	15.3	22.3	29.5	13
Cucumber	5.0	7.3	7.7	7.1	5.5	4.6	(2)
Tomato	5.6	5.9	6.3	5.8	3.9	2.7	(13)
Watermelon	12.1	11.8	12.2	11.8	21.3	8.9	(6)
Total	417.6	350.6	327.4	298.5	317.3	256.3	(9)

( ) = negative value, CAGR = compound annual growth rate.

Note: Numbers may not sum precisely because of rounding.

Source: Team analysis using data from the National Statistical Office of Mongolia.

2.2.1.1   Total Market Value

The estimated total value of Mongolia's vegetable market is summarized in Table 2. To estimate the total market value for vegetables in dollars, the apparent consumption volume for each type of vegetable was multiplied by the corresponding average retail price, where data was available, and divided by the respective year's mean togrog exchange rate. For some types of vegetables, the researchers were not able to find retail prices for respective years. In such cases, unit import prices were used and multiplied by the order of three, based on observed price differentiation between retail and import unit prices.

Table 2 shows the total market value of vegetables in dollars decreased, with a CAGR of –17% between 2012 and 2017, from $325 million in 2012 to $125 million in 2017. During this period, market values of onion, garlic, and watermelon showed a slight increase, while all other commonly consumed vegetables decreased. Potato market values decreased the most, with a CAGR of –25%, followed by carrots and turnips, with a CAGR of –19%. The vegetable market value on a togrog basis showed a more stable result, with a CAGR of –7%, compared to a –17% CAGR on a dollar basis. However, it still shows an overall decline in market value.

The following should be noted about the estimates in Table 2:

First, the estimates are based on the total volume of production of the selected vegetables at the farm gate multiplied by various prices at the retail level. This assumes that there is no reduction in the volume of vegetables between the farm and retail market due to spoilage or return and destruction of unsold product. It is likely that some percentage of farm gate production is subject to reduction for these reasons.

Second, the market estimate includes a selection of vegetables for which data on production, trade, and prices are available on a consistent basis. There are other vegetables produced for which data

Table 2: Estimated Vegetable Market Value, 2012–2017
($'000)

Item	2012	2013	2014	2015	2016	2017	CAGR (%)
Potato	189,345	116,541	88,271	115,978	81,652	44,063	(25)
Vegetables, specified	135,951	129,939	114,736	83,840	96,289	80,911	(10)
Cabbage	44,396	36,953	28,259	28,922	28,002	29,759	(8)
Carrot, turnip	65,429	54,875	49,090	29,318	44,968	22,905	(19)
Onion, garlic	12,091	22,166	19,484	9,599	13,353	16,525	6
Cucumber	4,392	5,781	6,385	5,013	3,985	3,221	(6)
Tomato	4,029	4,907	5,205	4,203	2,905	2,179	(12)
Watermelon	5,613	5,258	6,313	6,784	3,077	6,321	2
Total Market	**325,296**	**246,480**	**203,007**	**199,818**	**177,941**	**124,974**	**(17)**
$1.00 to MNT exchange rate	1,359	1,522	1,818	1,970	2,146	2,440	12
Total Market (MNT million)	**442,156**	**375,207**	**369,054**	**393,703**	**381,778**	**304,906**	**(7)**

( ) = negative value, CAGR = compound annual growth rate, MNT = Mongolian togrog.

Source: Team analysis using data from the National Statistical Office of Mongolia, the Mongolian Customs, and the MongolBank.

are not available on a consistent basis. For example, there is a significant and apparently fast-growing market for high-value leafy vegetables, especially in metropolitan Ulaanbaatar. Import data are available for a residual category of "other" imports that includes leafy vegetables, and imports of this category have grown from 7.0 kilotons (kt) in 2012 ($1.578 million) to 15.2 kt in 2017 ($3.261 million). Detailed statistics obtained by the consultants indicate that import volumes of products such as bok choy, eggplants, mushrooms, peppers, and spinach have increased at significantly higher rates than those of other more traditional vegetables, growing between 60% and 885%. Their unit values are generally higher than for traditional vegetables, but these values have fallen in recent years, suggesting fast growth in market demand and strong competition in pricing.

There is clearly a need to expand the coverage of vegetable production statistics to specifically provide data on leafy and nontraditional or specialty vegetables.

Finally, the table was based on the assumption that all vegetables produced at the farm gate are being sold at retail prices. However, some vegetables are sold to processors for conversion into processed vegetable products. This is discussed further in the value chain mapping analysis in section 3.1, but the volumes sold to processors are estimated to be only about 3% to 5% of total sales.

2.2.1.2 Local Field and Greenhouse Crops with Strong Projected Demand

There are approximately 30 varieties of vegetables grown in Mongolia.[6] Table 3 summarizes local field and/or greenhouse crops that are expected to increase in production in the next 5–6 years. It identifies the main geographic regions where these crops are produced, the current markets, and the storage approaches.

---

[6]   Action for Enterprise. 2014. *Value Chain Program Design in the Mongolian Vegetable Value Chain*. Arlington, VA. pp. 3 and 11.

Table 3: Production, Markets, and Storage of Local Field and Greenhouse Crops

Vegetables	Main Provinces and Production Methods	Markets and Storage Approaches
Leafy Green Celery Coriander Lettuce Spinach	Most leafy vegetables are grown in greenhouses in areas close to the cities of Darkhan, Erdenet, and Ulaanbaatar.	Sold in informal markets such as the Ulaanbaatar open markets and/or kiosks and wholesalers. Some cooperatives and producers sell directly to supermarkets and restaurants. These crops are perishable and, by the end of each September, the supply is diminished. Only a few entities that have winter greenhouses produce them during winter and spring and sell them informally to open markets or formally to supermarkets.
Beans Cucumber Pumpkin Sweet pepper Tomato Zucchini	These types of vegetable are normally produced in greenhouses. Individual farms produce these vegetables in greenhouses during summer. Larger-scale entities such as Atriin Shim, Devshil, Green City, Nogoon Sor, and others grow cucumbers and tomatoes from March to late September.	Sold in informal markets such as the Ulaanbaatar open markets and/or kiosks and wholesalers. Some cooperatives and producers sell directly to supermarkets and restaurants.
Potato	The main potato-growing *aimags* are Khovd, Selenge, and Tuv. Currently, most irrigation is provided by open water sources or hand wells using diesel water pumps and plastic portable pipes.	Some large-scale growers in Selenge and Tuv *aimags* sell potatoes to wholesalers who normally store them in rented warehouses. Those who have underground storage keep some potatoes until spring to sell at higher prices (approximately 50% higher).
Root Crops Beetroot Carrot Radish Turnip	Carrots, turnips, and other root crops are produced in all *aimags*. Zuunkharaa *soum* of Selenge *aimag* producers tend to specialize in cabbage and carrot production (*see discussion below re: cruciferous crops*). Radish is normally grown by small-scale farmers only during the summer period.	Individual growers store their root crops in underground storage, which is normally built below soil freezing depth (more than 4–5 meters). Farmers typically sell some produce in autumn and save some to sell in early spring.
Cruciferous Cabbage Broccoli Cauliflower	Cabbages are normally grown in open irrigated fields, mostly in the Zuunkharaa *soum* of Selenge *aimag*, but some experienced farmers grow them in greenhouses to sell in early summer. Broccoli and cauliflowers are normally grown in greenhouses, but not in as large quantities as carrots or cucumbers.	Cabbages are rarely stored by individual farmers, who sell their produce until the end of each November. From 2016, one supermarket chain has stored cabbages until March in a large-scale warehouse.
Allium Chinese garlic Garlic Onion Spring onion	These types of vegetable are very popular and are normally grown in open fields. Garlic is mainly produced in the western *aimags* such as Uvs and Zavkhan, as well as in the Zuunkharaa *soum* of Selenge *aimag*. Farmers are experienced in production of garlic, especially spring onions. Chinese garlic is not produced in large quantities, but only by small family farms near Ulaanbaatar City.	Onion and garlic are easily stored in underground storage. Garlic is mainly sold out by early November each year, but onions are sold all year-round.

continued on next page

Table 3 *continued*

Vegetables	Main Provinces and Production Methods	Markets and Storage Approaches
Berries Blackcurrant Sea buckthorn Strawberry	Sea buckthorn is grown in open fields, and growers in Khovd, Uvs, and Zavkhan *aimags* tend to grow it in large quantities for both commercial sales and export. Some larger-scale private entities also grow it along the Tuul River and near Ulaanbaatar City. Blackcurrants are mainly produced by farmers in Selenge and Tuv *aimags*, but not in as large quantities as sea buckthorn. Strawberries are grown by a few entities located in areas surrounding Ulaanbaatar City, who have appropriate greenhouse and irrigation facilities.	Supermarkets and open markets sell frozen sea buckthorn all year-round, but fresh berries are only sold during September and October. Some large-scale sea buckthorn producers (2–5 hectares) in Uvs *aimag* have their own facilities that produce sea buckthorn oils. Blackcurrants are sold fresh from late July to late August and are available at open markets. Most Mongolian-grown strawberries are formally traded through supermarkets. They are available at open markets only during late July–September.
Fruits Melon Watermelon	Watermelon and melon are mainly produced in open fields, mostly in Khovd and Selenge *aimags*. Some experienced entities produce watermelon and melon in greenhouses and supply them to target markets from July until late September.	Watermelon is transported in large quantities to Ulaanbaatar City and mainly sold informally to wholesalers or on major roads.

aimag = is a provincial administrative unit in Mongolia, *soum* = is a subprovincial administrative unit in Mongolia, which is equivalent to a district.

Source: Team analysis using field survey data.

2.2.1.3 Self-Sufficiency Rate of Domestic Production (Local Supply)

One strategy to reduce dependency on imported vegetable produce is to increase the self-sufficiency rate of domestic farm production. Official statistics indicate that the vegetable production self-sufficiency rate in Mongolia had improved between 2012 and 2017, with the exception of cabbage (Table 4). Due to several successful targeted projects implemented since 2000, domestic production of potato satisfies total demand with a 100% self-sufficiency rate. Tomatoes (CAGR of 14%) and watermelon (CAGR of 11%) production experienced the highest growth during 2012–2017.

Table 4: Vegetable Production Self-Sufficiency Rate, 2012–2017
(%)

Item	2012	2013	2014	2015	2016	2017	CAGR (%)
Potato	98.7	101.3	99.4	90.5	99.6	100.1	0
Vegetables, specified	51.8	52.5	52.4	53.3	54.1	66.9	5
Cabbage	36.9	47.1	43.9	38.6	40.4	33.6	(2)
Carrot, turnip	75.4	84.5	86.5	95.8	84.9	78.2	1
Onion, garlic	34.4	36.5	33.0	43.8	44.4	41.1	4
Cucumber	74.0	58.9	61.2	53.5	67.3	84.3	3
Tomato	37.5	42.4	38.1	32.8	56.4	73.6	14
Watermelon	52.9	45.8	51.6	55.1	31.0	91.0	11

( ) = negative value, CAGR = compound annual growth rate.

Source: Team analysis using data from the National Statistical Office of Mongolia.

2.2.1.4   Valuation of Market Sizes for Promising Crops in Ulaanbaatar and Other Cities

Vegetable use and consumption is not uniform across Mongolia. City dwellers consume, on average, 27% more potatoes and 70% more vegetables annually compared to rural residents. For potatoes and vegetables combined, city dwellers consume, on average, 42% more than rural residents. Pastoralist herders consume a negligible amount of greens and vegetables throughout their lifetime. Moreover, most large-scale institutional buyers and consumers are heavily concentrated in urban areas.

Therefore, a very conservative method to calculate the potential market size for potato and vegetable consumption in Ulaanbaatar and other cities can be based on population and per capita intake estimates for respective populations. Population data for 2012–2017 are shown in Table 5.

Table 5: Urban and Rural Population of Mongolia, 2012–2017

Population	2012	2013	2014	2015	2016	2017
Urban (all cities, including UB)	1,926,625	1,995,712	1,990,321	2,096,180	2,131,823	2,146,716
Rural	941,119	934,565	1,005,628	961,598	988,112	1,031,183
UB City	1,318,130	1,372,042	1,362,974	1,396,288	1,440,447	1,462,973
Total Population	**2,867,744**	**2,930,277**	**2,995,949**	**3,057,778**	**3,119,935**	**3,177,899**

UB = Ulaanbaatar.
Source: National Statistical Office of Mongolia.

Table 6 summarizes the average per capita annual vegetable consumption in urban and rural areas during 2012–2016. Table 6 and 7 demonstrate the considerable difference in vegetable consumption between urban and rural residents.

Table 6: Urban and Rural Per Capita Average Annual Vegetable Consumption, 2012–2016
(kilogram)

Area	Item	2012	2013	2014	2015	2016
Urban	Potato	40.8	43.2	39.6	37.2	36.0
	Vegetables	28.8	31.2	30.0	28.8	25.2
Rural	Potato	36.0	31.2	31.2	27.6	30.0
	Vegetables	16.8	15.6	18.0	16.8	18.0
Ulaanbaatar	Potato	44.9	44.7	42.0	39.8	36.6
	Vegetables	33.3	34.6	32.6	30.3	26.6

Source: National Statistical Office of Mongolia.

Table 7: Difference between Urban and Rural Per Capita Average Annual Vegetable Consumption, 2012–2016 (%)

Item	2012	2013	2014	2015	2016	Average
Potato	13	38	27	35	20	27
Vegetables	71	100	67	71	40	70
Total	**32**	**59**	**41**	**49**	**28**	**42**

Source: National Statistical Office of Mongolia.

According to the NSO, in 2017, nationwide annual demand reached 129.0 kt for potatoes and 184.2 kt for vegetables, up from 9.1 kt for potatoes and 12.9 kt for vegetables in 2013, while combined supply from state harvest and imports was 123.0 kt for potatoes and 157.3 kt for vegetables (Table 8).[7] This indicates the need for enhanced production of these two food groups.

Based on this data, the annual per capita consumption of potatoes was 40.6 kilograms (kg) (or 111.3 g/day), and vegetables 52.0 kg (142.4 g/day), lower than the recommended quantities of 120 g/day for potatoes and 260 g/day for vegetables by the Ministry of Health (footnote 1). Given this, vegetable production needs to increase by around 45%, while potato production currently almost covers consumption requirements.

Table 8: Nationwide Consumption of Potato and Vegetables, 2017

	Total Harvest (ton)	Total Imported (ton)	Total Supply (ton)	Percent of Import in Total Supply (%)	Resident Population	Annual Consumption per Capita (kg)	Daily Consumption per Capita (g)
Potato	121,808.5	1,144.7	122,953.2	0.9	3,026,905	40.6	111.3
Vegetables	82,102.0	75,234.0	157,336.0	47.8		52.0	142.4

g = gram, kg = kilogram.
Source: National Statistical Office of Mongolia.

The average potential market sizes of potatoes and other vegetables, expressed by volume in kt, are presented in Table 9, using as bases for calculation the apparent consumption figures for 2012–2017 presented in Table 1.

---

[7]   Government of Mongolia, National Statistical Office. 2017. *Indicators for Food Security Statistics 2016*. Ulaanbaatar.

Table 9: Average Potential Market Size of Vegetables, by Volume
('000 ton)

Item	2012	2013	2014	2015	2016	2017	CAGR (%)	Average
Potato	249.1	189.1	162.4	180.9	166.0	121.6	(13)	178.2
Vegetables, specified	168.5	161.5	165.0	117.6	151.3	134.7	(4)	149.8
Cabbage	54.7	43.7	42.6	39.9	41.3	45.2	(4)	44.6
Carrot, turnip	75.1	67.3	67.7	37.7	57.0	43.7	(10)	58.1
Onion, garlic	16.0	25.5	28.5	15.3	22.3	29.5	13	22.8
Cucumber	5.0	7.3	7.7	7.1	5.5	4.6	(2)	6.2
Tomato	5.6	5.9	6.3	5.8	3.9	2.7	(13)	5.0
Watermelon	12.1	11.8	12.2	11.8	21.3	8.9	(6)	13.0
Total	**417.6**	**350.6**	**327.4**	**298.5**	**317.3**	**256.3**	**(9)**	**328.0**

( ) = negative value, CAGR = compound annual growth rate.
Note: Numbers may not sum precisely because of rounding.
Source: Team analysis using data from the National Statistical Office of Mongolia.

Apparent consumption in 2017 was considerably lower for each vegetable (except onion and garlic) than in the previous 5 years. For the purposes of this market study, it was assumed that by 2020, apparent consumption would have increased to the average volume as shown in Table 10.

While this might be considered ambitious, it must be remembered that consumption declines since 2012 have been driven largely by the more than half reduction in potato production. There is no data on production of some of the higher-value vegetables, such as leafy greens, for which imports have been growing strongly. Taken together, these could see overall vegetable consumption return to the average level of recent years.

Table 10: Estimation of Potential Consumption of Vegetables, 2018–2020
('000 ton)

Item	2017	2018	2019	2020	Estimated CAGR (%)
Potato	121.6	138.1	156.9	178.2	14
Vegetables, specified	134.7	144.9	156.5	169.4	8
Cabbage	45.2	45.0	44.8	44.6	0
Carrot, turnip	43.7	48.1	52.8	58.1	10
Onion, garlic	29.5	33.3	37.6	42.5	13
Cucumber	4.6	5.1	5.6	6.2	10
Tomato	2.7	3.3	4.1	5.0	23
Watermelon	8.9	10.1	11.5	13.0	14
Total	**256.3**	**283.1**	**313.4**	**347.6**	**11**

CAGR = compound annual growth rate.
Notes:
1. Assumptions include (i) by 2020, the market size for each vegetable, except onions and garlic, will reach at least the average volume of apparent consumption observed during 2015–2020; and (ii) market size for onions and garlic will increase by 11% per year during 2018–2020.
2. Numbers may not sum precisely because of rounding.
Source: Team analysis using data from the National Statistical Office of Mongolia.

By weighing the population estimates by per capita consumption based on the assumption that 68% of the population living in urban areas consume 27% of potatoes and 70% of vegetables, the total potential urban and rural market size volumes can be estimated as shown in Table 11.

Table 11: Valuation of Market Size for Potato and Vegetables in Urban and Rural Areas, by Volume, 2018–2020
('000 ton)

Item	2018	2019	2020
Urban			
Potato	100.2	113.8	129.2
Selected vegetables	113.0	122.0	132.1
Total Urban	**213.2**	**235.7**	**261.3**
Rural			
Potato	38.0	43.1	49.0
Selected vegetables	31.9	34.5	37.3
Total Rural	**69.9**	**77.6**	**86.3**

Note: Numbers may not sum precisely because of rounding.
Source: National Statistical Office of Mongolia.

2.2.2   Relevance of Food Safety Assurance and Quality Standards

Mongolia has a number of laws and regulations governing vegetable production and food safety. Of particular relevance are the National Security Concept of Mongolia (which discusses human security and food security), the State Policy on Food and Agriculture, the Food Law of Mongolia, and the Law on Food Products' Safety. Also relevant are the Law on Hygiene, the Law on Standardization and Accreditation, and the Law on Agriculture. ADB has supported food safety work through several technical assistance (TA) and lending projects.[8] There are also several related food standards.

In 2015, the World Bank observed that Mongolian food products were of poor hygiene standard and, therefore, of low quality and value. It stated that improving food safety systems and product quality would help to expand markets and improve sales and price levels (footnote 3). It recommended that Mongolia should

■ adopt the four-level system recommended by the Food and Agriculture Organization (FAO) of the United Nations that would address (i) food safety regulations and guidelines; (ii) risk management issues in the food chain; (iii) inspection and enforcement; and (iv) training, studies, and other support work;

---

[8]   ADB. 2015. *Report and Recommendation of the President to the Board of Directors: Proposed Loan to Mongolia for the Regional Upgrades of Sanitary and Phytosanitary Measures for Trade Project.* Manila; and ADB. 2016. *Technical Assistance for Strengthening International Food Safety Standards in Agricultural Value Chains in the Central Asia Regional Economic Cooperation Member Countries.* Manila.

- ensure the implementation of food safety laws, policies, and regulations consistent with the *Codex Alimentarius*, the global framework for food safety regulation and the standard on which international market access is based;

- make public investments in the inspection system;

- provide TA and credit for upgrading technology and processes in private sector food companies to adopt Hazard Analysis and Critical Control Points (HACCP), Good Manufacturing Practices (GMP), and Good Hygiene Practices (GHP), as well as trace back systems;

- introduce the On-Farm Food Safety (OFFS) system to ensure the quality and safety of raw materials; and

- provide training and technical support to actors throughout the food system so that they understand (i) the requirements of the food safety laws and regulations, and (ii) how to properly apply them within their own facilities and farms.

Placing a value on the benefits of food safety and nutrition is one of the most important aspects of food quality assurance programs. The major benefit of a safer and more nutritious food supply accrues directly to consumers in the form of better health. A higher-quality food supply may allow consumers to more easily maintain their health, protect themselves against external health hazards, and rehabilitate their health in case of impairment. This, in turn, should reduce costs to the health-care system. Food companies can also benefit from assuring higher quality, for example, by attaining a better reputation with consumers, a longer shelf life for their products, and better access to foreign markets.

While there is no consensus on the most appropriate method of measuring the value of the benefits of food safety, several methods are available.

One approach is to measure the cost of illness (or avoided cost from, e.g., illness, death, pain, and suffering). This approach is considered to be a more reliable and conservative measure of benefits. Another is the contingent valuation and experimental markets approach, which measures customers' willingness to pay for specific safety attributions. Conjoint analysis examines consumers' preferences for products with enhanced safety or nutritional features. The most direct method of placing value is by comparing the differences between prices paid in markets for products based on different safety and nutrition characteristics. A liability cost approach is a measure of avoidable or potentially avoidable costs. A final approach is to measure the benefits of improved access to foreign markets through quality improvement or the cost of reduced access.

Studies show that consumers are willing to pay more for products that present a lower risk to their health.[9] However, consumers in Mongolia do not have the means to judge the quality and safety of the food products they consume. The United States has adopted quality signaling (labels) to improve the markets for nutritional quality. Such action not only informs and helps customers evaluate product quality, but also eventually reduces asymmetric information in the market, and potentially adds value to the product price. In economic theory, asymmetric information refers to the notion

---

[9]   J.A. Caswell. 1998. Valuing the Benefits and Costs of Improved Food Safety and Nutrition. *Australian Journal of Agricultural and Resource Economics.* 42 (4). pp. 409–424.

that one party possesses unequal and imbalanced information (e.g., quality of the seeds, whether the vegetables are organic). Reducing asymmetric information by providing information will give the end-customers confidence to purchase directly from farmers. Bulk buyers, such as retailers or institutions, will also collaborate with smallholder and individual farmers directly if their standards are met. The application of information and communication technology has shown high potential to achieve marketing to premium customers and reduction of food safety risks. Farmers have little access to wholesale price information and low awareness on value-added opportunities and marketing. The application of network-connected information and communication technology along the entire value chain from production to marketing would enable market access through a two-way automated information exchange system between producers and consumers. It provides consumers with food safety-related product information, while producers get access to market information.

During the field research for the market study, issues of food safety assurance and quality standards were raised with several representative stakeholders along the value chain. This information is summarized in Table 12, as indicative approaches used by some stakeholders.

Table 12: Examples of Food Safety Practices Along the Value Chain

Type of Organization	Comments Regarding Food Safety Assurance and Quality Standards
Retailer	**Food safety.** The company was certified in March 2017 (International Organization for Standardization [ISO] standards 9001, 14001, and 18001). They use a checklist for suppliers and have an inspection system (annual audit of storage warehouses and/or fields).
	Specification. In general, yes—e.g., potatoes should weigh 120–220 grams, and not be crushed or eaten by bugs or insects. No requirement for color since potatoes grown from seeds from the People's Republic of China tend to be pale yellow, while those grown from some Mongolian seeds are a deeper yellow.
Processor	**Quality and food safety.** A local branch of the General Agency for Specialized Inspection does soil inspection and monitoring of pesticides for a fee.
Hypermarket Chain	**Storing and quality standards.** There are standards for the warehouse and for storing vegetables in warehouses. Quality requirements include size, variety, cleanliness, and freshness.
	Specification. Before farmers are approved to supply products, their produce specifications are included in the contract (such as minimum and/or maximum size).
Hotel	**Specification.** In general, yes.
	Food safety. Hygiene specialist does checks of kitchen for quality of supplied products.
	Warehouse inspection. No system.

Source: Team analysis using field survey data.

As a general observation, Mongolian supermarket chains tend not to engage small farmers as direct suppliers. One of the reasons for this is the perception that customer demand is high, and the farmers cannot meet the quality requirements (which include food safety). Therefore, the supermarket chains buy most vegetable supplies from large suppliers, wholesalers, or importers.

It is relevant to note that most Mongolian vegetable support programs and policies are focused mainly on the volume and scope of production, technology and know-how, and diversification, among others. However, farmers, especially smallholder farmers, face challenges with marketing and selling their products. This eventually leads to more benefits from the value chain accruing to handlers and/or intermediaries. To achieve the maximum benefits for farmers and consumers, farmers and related institutions need to add more value to their products and eliminate other costs incurred in delivering the product to end-customers.

2.3 Supply Analysis

2.3.1 Market Size: Where Is Produce Grown, How, and in What Quantity?

Mongolia's main vegetable production regions are Bulgan, Khentii, Selenge, and Tuv *aimags*, where small-scale farmers mainly grow vegetables, including cabbage, carrot, cucumber, garlic, onion, potato, tomato, turnip, and watermelon. According to the NSO, in 2016, Mongolia had 17,415 small-scale and part-time smallholder farmers and/or vegetable growers.[10] The following *aimags* and city had the most growers: Selenge (4,022), Tuv (1,850), Ulaanbaatar City (1,699), and Darkhan-Uul (957).

The supply of vegetables and potatoes is determined by both local production and imported product. In 2016, the total cultivated area of potato crops was estimated at about 14,600 hectares (ha), from which 153.5 kt were harvested. The cultivated area for vegetable production was about 8,300 ha, from which 93.4 kt was harvested.[11]

Based on the consulting team's investigations, local producers tend to have limited knowledge or understanding of who are likely to be the consumers of their produce, how much of their products potential customers may use on an annual or seasonal basis, and what level of quality customers demand. In addition, these farmers lack institutional capacity to self-organize and undertake collective action to introduce innovative marketing strategies and technology transfer.

2.3.2 Supply Analysis: What Vegetables and Where From?

2.3.2.1 What Vegetables?

A pilot survey conducted in March 2018 shows that the assortment and availability of vegetables offered through retail channels in Ulaanbaatar have expanded considerably over the years. The survey covered vegetable stalls at supermarkets, wholesale stores, and retail markets. It counted over 50 different types of vegetables and greens including, but not limited to, avocado, baby spring garlic, bean sprouts, beech, bok choy, bottle gourd, broccoli, brussels sprouts, cabbage, mini cabbage, carrot, cauliflower, celery, chili, corn, cucumber, eggplant, garlic, ginger, green leaf lettuce, iceberg lettuce, kale, leek, brown mushroom, enoki mushroom, white button mushroom, onion, spring onion, parsley, pepper, potato, sweet potato, pumpkin, radish, spinach, tomato, and turnip.

To determine the market size and undertake a demand and supply analysis for vegetable production in Mongolia, the most commonly grown and consumed vegetables (cabbage, carrot, cucumber, garlic, onion, potato, tomato, turnip, and watermelon) were studied. These were identified based partly on the availability of reliable statistical data covering the 2012–2017 period and mostly on volumes produced, imported, and consumed.

---

[10]   Government of Mongolia, National Statistical Office. 2017. *Mongolian Statistical Yearbook 2016*. Ulaanbaatar.
[11]   Government of Mongolia, MOFALI. 2016. *Statistics Annual Report 2016*. Ulaanbaatar.

2.3.2.2   In What Quantities?

Farm production volumes of common vegetables harvested in Mongolia in 2012–2017 are shown in Table 13.[12] Aggregated farm production data for potatoes and other vegetables are shown, along with individual data for cabbage, carrot, cucumber, garlic, onion, tomato, turnip, and watermelon production, the sum of which is shown as percentage of the total. These common vegetables comprised 92%–97% of all vegetables produced in Mongolia during 2012–2017, as measured by official statistics.

Domestic vegetable farm production decreased from 344.9 kt to 203.9 kt, or by 41% between 2012 and 2017 (a 10% decrease in CAGR). Potato is the main vegetable grown in Mongolia, comprising 65% of all vegetables or 143.0 kt per year, on average. From 2012 to 2017, potato production decreased from 245.9 kt to 121.8 kt (CAGR of –13%), while vegetable production decreased from 99.0 kt to 82.1 kt (CAGR of –4%). Cucumber, garlic, onion, and watermelon farm production increased during the years analyzed. Garlic and onion production particularly showed significant growth compared to other peer categories, exhibiting a CAGR of 17%.

Table 13: Vegetable Farm Production, by Volume, 2012–2017
('000 ton)

Item	2012	2013	2014	2015	2016	2017	CAGR (%)
Potato	245.9	191.6	161.5	163.8	165.3	121.8	(13)
Vegetables, All	99.0	101.9	104.9	72.3	94.5	82.1	(4)
Cabbage	20.2	20.6	18.7	15.4	16.7	15.2	(6)
Carrot, turnip	56.6	56.9	58.6	36.1	48.4	34.2	(10)
Onion, garlic	5.5	9.3	9.4	6.7	9.9	12.1	17
Cucumber	3.7	4.3	4.7	3.8	3.7	3.9	1
Tomato	2.1	2.5	2.4	1.9	2.2	2.0	(1)
Watermelon	6.4	5.4	6.3	6.5	6.6	8.1	5
Total vegetables, specified	94.5	99.0	100.1	70.4	87.5	75.5	(4)
% of Specified in All	95%	97%	95%	97%	93%	92%	(1)
Total	**344.9**	**293.5**	**266.4**	**236.1**	**259.8**	**203.9**	**(10)**

( ) = negative value, CAGR = compound annual growth rate.
Source: National Statistical Office of Mongolia.

---

[12]   There is a slight variance between the data about total vegetables included in Table 13 and Table 14. It is understood that this is due to rounding differences.

Table 14 shows the proportion of potatoes and vegetables harvested compared with cereals and fodder crops over the same period.

Table 14: Potato, Vegetables, Cereals, and Fodder Crop Production, by Harvest Volume, 2012–2017
('000 ton)

Total Harvested	2012	2013	2014	2015	2016	2017
Potato	245.9	191.6	161.5	163.8	165.3	121.8
Vegetables	98.9	101.8	104.8	72.3	94.4	82.1
Cereals	479.3	387.0	518.8	216.3	483.5	238.1
Fodder Crop	46.2	42.6	44.3	49.2	53.4	47.9

Source: Ministry of Food, Agriculture and Light Industry.

Potato and vegetable production by all producers, including smallholder farmers, within the four *aimags* selected for the ADB project (i.e., Darkhan-Uul, Selenge, Tuv, and Uvs) were the largest nationwide in 2017, with a total of 82.1 kt of potato (67%) and 50.8 kt of vegetables (62%). Among the project *aimags*, Tuv had the highest production potential in potato farming (41.7 kt, 34%), and Selenge produced the largest portion of vegetables (30.8 kt, 37.5%) (Table 15).

Project-focus *soums* (i.e., Bornuur in Tuv, Orkhon in Darkhan-Uul, Ulaangom in Uvs, and Yeruu in Selenge) together accounted for 6%–10% of total domestic potato production and 11%–18% of domestic vegetable production between 2014 and 2016, as shown in Table 16 and 17. This is quite a remarkable contribution for only four *soums*, considering that 318 out of 330 *soums* reported potato or vegetable production in 2016, albeit very low in most cases.

At their peak, Orkhon produced 15.7 kt of potato and vegetables in 2014, while, in 2015, Bornuur's farm production amounted to 14.6 kt. Between 2014 and 2016, potato production in the four *soums* decreased, with a CAGR of –23%, and vegetable production as well, with a CAGR of –5%, representing a total reduction in production, with a CAGR of –13%.

Tables 18 and 19 show vegetable plantation areas and the yield for respective years. The highest yield in potato production was achieved in 2015 in Bornuur with 16.6 tons/ha, while Yeruu led vegetable production with a yield of 14.8 tons/ha in 2014.

Table 15: Total Yield of Potato and Vegetables, by *Aimag*, 2017

	Item	Potato		Vegetables	
		Yield (ton)	Total Production (%)	Yield (ton)	Total Production (%)
Nationwide		**121,808.5**	**100.00**	**82,102.0**	**100.00**
Aimags	Arkhangai	2,507.7	2.06	754.0	0.92
	Bayankhongor	1,547.9	1.27	794.3	0.97
	Bayan-Ulgii	3,254.7	2.67	1,612.3	1.96
	Bulgan	3,623.0	2.97	993.5	1.21
	Darkhan-Uul	8,605.2	7.06	13,665.8	16.64
	Dornod	1,323.8	1.09	649.0	0.79
	Dornogovi	100.3	0.08	346.5	0.42
	Dundgovi	169.1	0.14	77.2	0.09
	Govi-Altai	831.4	0.68	371.1	0.45
	Govisumber	100.6	0.08	140.7	0.17
	Khentii	2,966.4	2.44	2,054.8	2.50
	Khovd	9,462.2	7.77	10,806.0	13.16
	Khuvsgul	2,793.5	2.29	1,846.9	2.25
	Orkhon	2,493.2	2.05	2,647.2	3.22
	Selenge	28,557.9	23.44	30,803.0	37.52
	Sukhbaatar	572.4	0.47	255.9	0.31
	Tuv	41,727.8	34.26	3,227.5	3.93
	Ulaanbaatar	1,361.6	1.12	4,081.5	4.97
	Umnugovi	544.3	0.45	719.7	0.88
	Uvs	3,220.5	2.64	3,114.9	3.79
	Uvurkhangai	3,917.6	3.22	2,020.0	2.46
	Zavkhan	2,127.5	1.75	1,120.2	1.36

Notes:
1. An *aimag* is a provincial administrative unit in Mongolia.
2. Numbers may not sum precisely, and percentages may not total 100%, because of rounding.

Source: National Statistical Office of Mongolia.

Table 16: Vegetable Farm Production Volume in the Project Soums, 2014–2016
(ton)

Item	Yeruu			Orkhon			Bornuur			Ulaangom			Total of All Four Soums		
	2014	2015	2016	2014	2015	2016	2014	2015	2016	2014	2015	2016	2014	2015	2016
Potato	1,726	711	868	2,983	885	3,731	10,798	12,416	3,207	1,278	1,968	2,120	16,785	15,979	9,925
Vegetables, All	1,713	763	1,016	12,806	2,983	10,890	3,366	2,171	3,207	1,381	1,900	2,146	19,265	7,817	17,259
Cabbage	173	84	92	504	47	82	857	697	731	335	473	514	1,870	1,301	1,420
Carrot	759	266	451	6,123	814	6,462	1,788	665	1,607	292	438	533	8,962	2,183	9,052
Turnip	164	170	156	1,064	451	1,605	329	692	392	382	539	569	1,939	1,852	2,722
Onion	189	64	112	2,294	784	1,577	36	14	188	46	55	60	2,564	917	1,937
Garlic				33						2	2	3	35	2	3
Cucumber	182	44	87	743	770	690		8		100	92	91	1,025	914	868
Tomato	110	20	27	104	1	4		1		28	34	35	242	57	65
Watermelon	22	20	36	81		13				1			104	20	49
Total vegetables, specified	1,599	669	961	10,947	2,866	10,433	3,010	2,077	2,918	1,184	1,634	1,804	16,741	7,246	16,115
Total	**3,439**	**1,474**	**1,884**	**15,788**	**3,868**	**14,621**	**14,164**	**14,586**	**6,414**	**2,659**	**3,868**	**4,265**	**36,050**	**23,796**	**27,184**

Notes:
1. *Soum* is a subprovincial administrative unit in Mongolia, which is equivalent to a district.
2. Numbers may not sum precisely because of rounding.

Source: National Statistical Office of Mongolia.

Table 17: Potato and Vegetable Production Volume in the Project Soums, Share in the National Total, 2014–2016
(ton)

Item		2014	2015	2016	CAGR (%)
National Farm Production	Potato	161,500	163,800	165,300	1
	Vegetables	104,900	72,300	94,500	(5)
	Total	**266,400**	**236,100**	**259,800**	**(1)**
Four Soums Farm Production	Potato	16,785	15,979	9,925	(23)
	Vegetables	19,265	7,817	17,259	(5)
	Total	**36,050**	**23,796**	**27,184**	**(13)**
Share of Four Soums in National Production	Potato	10.4%	9.8%	6.0%	(24)
	Vegetables	18.4%	10.8%	18.3%	0
	Total	**13.5%**	**10.1%**	**10.5%**	**(12)**

( ) = negative value, CAGR = compound annual growth rate.
Note: *Soum* is a subprovincial administrative unit in Mongolia, which is equivalent to a district.
Source: National Statistical Office of Mongolia.

Table 18: Vegetable Plantation Areas in the Project Soums, 2014–2016
(hectare)

Item	Yeruu			Orkhon			Bornuur			Ulaangom			Total of All Four Soums		
	2014	2015	2016	2014	2015	2016	2014	2015	2016	2014	2015	2016	2014	2015	2016
Potato	150	71	74	201	110	297	750	750	800	78	131	141	1,178	1,062	1,312
Vegetables, All	116	168	70	1,067	759	1,389	268	209	252	102	144	151	1,553	1,280	1,862
Cabbage	13	11	7	23	1	4	30	30	34	22	30	32	88	72	77
Carrot	37	27	25	510	420	644	166	72	131	24	35	36	737	554	836
Turnip	18	20	13	204	155	496	30	41	40	25	34	34	277	250	582
Onion	13	88	9	152	97	119	12	12	20	7	10	10	184	207	158
Garlic				2		1				3	5	5	5	5	6
Cucumber	13	5	7	35	42	68		1		6	6	6	54	54	81
Tomato	11	3	2	5	1	1		1		2	2	3	18	6	6
Watermelon	2	3	2	1		3							3	3	5
Total vegetables, specified	107	155	65	934	716	1,335	238	157	225	87	120	125	1,365	1,148	1,750
Total	**266**	**239**	**144**	**1,268**	**869**	**1,686**	**1,018**	**959**	**1,052**	**179**	**275**	**292**	**2,731**	**2,342**	**3,174**

Notes:
1. *Soum* is a subprovincial administrative unit in Mongolia, which is equivalent to a district.
2. Numbers may not sum precisely because of rounding.

Source: National Statistical Office of Mongolia.

Table 19: Vegetable Yield in the Project Soums, 2014–2016
(hectare)

Item	Yeruu			Orkhon			Bornuur			Ulaangom			Total of All Four Soums		
	2014	2015	2016	2014	2015	2016	2014	2015	2016	2014	2015	2016	2014	2015	2016
Potato	11.5	10.0	11.8	14.9	8.0	12.6	14.4	16.6	4.0	16.4	15.0	15.0	14.2	15.0	7.6
Vegetables, All	14.8	4.5	14.5	12.0	3.9	7.8	12.6	10.4	12.7	13.6	13.2	14.2	12.4	6.1	9.3
Cabbage	13.3	8.0	14.2	21.5	46.5	20.1	28.6	22.9	21.4	15.4	16.0	16.0	21.2	18.2	18.5
Carrot	20.5	10.0	18.0	12.0	1.9	10.0	10.8	9.2	12.2	12.3	12.4	15.0	12.2	3.9	10.8
Turnip	9.1	8.5	12.0	5.2	2.9	3.2	11.0	16.9	9.9	15.4	15.9	17.0	7.0	7.4	4.7
Onion	14.5	0.7	11.9	15.1	8.1	13.3	3.0	1.2	9.4	6.7	5.7	6.1	14.0	4.4	12.3
Garlic				16.4						0.6	0.5	0.5	7.4	0.5	0.5
Cucumber	14.0	9.0	12.1	21.0	18.3	10.2		8.0		18.0	15.9	14.8	19.0	17.0	10.7
Tomato	10.0	8.2	11.7	19.6	1.1	2.7		2.0		17.6	22.6	13.3	13.5	10.2	10.5
Watermelon	11.2	8.0	18.0	59.1		4.8							31.0	8.0	10.5
Total vegetables, specified	14.9	4.3	14.7	11.7	4.0	7.8	12.6	13.2	13.0	13.6	13.6	14.5	12.3	6.3	9.2
Total	**12.9**	**6.2**	**13.1**	**12.5**	**4.5**	**8.7**	**13.9**	**15.2**	**6.1**	**14.8**	**14.0**	**14.6**	**13.2**	**10.2**	**8.6**

Notes:
1. *Soum* is a subprovincial administrative unit in Mongolia, which is equivalent to a district.
2. Numbers may not sum precisely because of rounding.

Source: National Statistical Office of Mongolia.

The most common vegetables grown in the four project *soums* are beetroot, carrot, cucumber, onion, pepper, potato, tomato, and turnip. Less common vegetables (and fruit) grown in these areas are bean snaps, broccoli, lettuce, pea, and strawberry. Ulaangom has been designated for seed production of some root crops such as beetroot, carrot, onion, and turnip since socialist times due to its amenable climate and support from the Ulaangom branch of the Plant Science and Agricultural Research Institute (PSARI). Ulaangom's seed production is undertaken by farmers associated with the Mongolian Farmer Association for Rural Development (MFARD) and supported by the PSARI and the Inclusive and Sustainable Vegetable Production and Marketing (VEGI) Project of the Swiss Agency for Development and Cooperation (SDC). Their total annual seed production is 3.5 tons of carrots, 3 tons of turnips, 1.5 tons of beetroots, and 0.08 tons of cabbages. Together with other Ulaangom farms, total seed production of root crops is about 10 tons, which covers 95% of national demand.

The lack of management policy, poor mechanization, and inadequate financial situation during the years of agricultural privatization have placed these four project *soums* in a vulnerable position, with insufficient production capacity to supply market demand. In addition, enhanced crop planting, improved water and soil usage, and crop residue management have not been well established in each *soum*. Enhanced crop planting based on an estimation of plant-growing days and seed- and/or seedling-planting dates has not been in practice for many years. Determining plant-growing days for vegetables is important for improving production capacity.

To determine vegetable farming capacity, growing degree days (GDDs) of the common and the less common vegetables (and fruit), as well as potential introduction of some new vegetables in these four project *soums*, were examined based on the lower development threshold (LDT) of the vegetables (Table 20). The LDT is the temperature, expressed in degrees Celsius (°C), below which plant growth becomes negligible. The GDDs were estimated using the last 10 years (2008–2017) of daily temperature data obtained from Mongolia's National Agency for Meteorology and Environmental Monitoring. Among the four project soums, the GDD scores of all vegetables tested in Ulaangom were the highest.

LDT and GDD data also indicate the need for an isolated environment (i.e., greenhouse) to sustain growth of some vegetables and fruit, such as cucumber, eggplant, pepper, snap beans, tomato, and watermelon.

Most vegetable farmers and smallholder farmers of the selected four *soums* rely on their experience rather than scientific knowledge to run their businesses. Determining plant growth start dates and plant growth lengths based on the LDT of vegetables would enhance production potential and improve competitiveness in the market.

Table 21 shows the planting date and plant growth length of open field-grown common and new vegetables for the four selected *soums*. This information shows that it is possible to extend the growth season by 2–3 weeks beyond current assumptions. The planting date of each vegetable, according to the local climate conditions described below, will help farmers and smallholder farmers plan and design their businesses and access points to the existing markets accordingly.

Table 20: Summary of Growing Degree Days of Vegetables Cultivated in the Project *Soums*

Item		LDT (°C)	Growing Degree Days			
			Yeruu	Ulaangom	Bornuur	Orkhon
Common Vegetables	Onion	1.7	2,190.01	2,312.03	2,253.61	2,280.24
	Carrot	3.3	1,878.18	1,999.64	1,938.78	1,979.40
	Potato	4.4	1,682.72	1,799.96	1,740.59	1,790.31
	Beet	4.4	1,682.72	1,799.96	1,740.59	1,790.31
	Tomato	10.0	857.42	924.98	891.28	984.13
	Pepper	10.0	857.42	924.98	891.28	984.13
	Cucumber	12.8	536.82	594.48	553.69	668.52
Less Common Vegetables	Strawberry	3.9	1,778.62	1,898.73	1,838.90	1,883.57
	Broccoli	4.4	1,682.72	1,799.96	1,740.59	1,790.31
	Lettuce	4.4	1,682.72	1,799.96	1,740.59	1,790.31
	Pea	4.4	1,682.72	1,799.96	1,740.59	1,790.31
	Snap bean	10.0	857.42	924.98	891.28	984.13
New Vegetables	Watermelon	12.8	536.82	594.48	553.69	668.52
	Eggplant	15.6	269.79	316.54	277.86	389.83
	Asparagus	4.4	1,682.72	1,799.96	1,740.59	1,790.31
	Collard	4.4	1,682.72	1,799.96	1,740.59	1,790.31
	Squash	7.2	1,244.52	1,327.11	1,287.23	1,364.03
	Muskmelon	10.0	857.42	924.98	891.28	984.13
	Sweet corn	10.0	857.42	924.98	891.28	984.13
	Okra	15.6	269.79	316.54	277.86	389.83
	Sweet potato	15.6	269.79	316.54	277.86	389.83

LDT = lower development threshold.

Notes:

1. *Soum* is a subprovincial administrative unit in Mongolia, which is equivalent to a district.
2. The LDT is the temperature, in degrees Celsius (°C), below which growth of each plant is negligible.

Source: Mongolia's National Agency for Meteorology and Environmental Monitoring.

Table 21: Planting Start Date and Growth Length of Vegetables Cultivated in the Project *Soums*

Item		Yeruu		Ulaangom		Bornuur		Orkhon	
		Planting Start Date	Growth Length	Planting Start Date	Growth Length	Planting Start Date	Growth Length	Planting Start Date	Growth Length
Common Vegetables	Onion	Apr 06–11	192	Apr 11–12	187	Apr 11–12	188	Apr 11–12	179
	Carrot	Apr 11–12	183	Apr 12–13	182	Apr 11–12	180	Apr 11–12	175
	Potato	Apr 12–25	177	Apr 13–14	177	Apr 12–13	179	Apr 12–16	165
	Beet	Apr 12–25	177	Apr 13–14	177	Apr 12–13	179	Apr 12–16	165
Less Common Vegetables	Strawberry	Apr 12–21	179	Apr 12–13	181	Apr 12–20	179	Apr 11–12	168
	Broccoli	Apr 12–25	177	Apr 13–14	177	Apr 12–13	179	Apr 12–16	165
	Lettuce	Apr 12–25	177	Apr 13–14	177	Apr 12–16	179	Apr 12–26	165
	Pea	Apr 12–25	177	Apr 13–14	177	Apr 12–20	179	Apr 12–26	165
	Snap bean	May 15–17	128	May 13–14	129	Apr 28–May 14	146	Apr 28–May 16	132
New Vegetables	Watermelon	May 16–30	112	May 16–29	115	May 15–29	126	May 15–29	111
	Collard	Apr 25–26	164	Apr 13–14	177	Apr 12–13	179	Apr 12–26	165
	Squash	Apr 27–28	152	Apr 25–26	152	Apr 27–28	151	Apr 27–28	145
	Muskmelon	May 15–20	128	Apr 26–May 13	146	May 12–14	134	Apr 28–May 09	132
	Sweet corn	May 15–20	128	May 13–14	129	May 12–13	134	May 01–14	129
	Okra	May 25–Jun 10	99	May 30–31	94	May 25–30	101	May 25–29	98
	Sweet potato	May 25–Jun 10	93	May 30–31	94	May 25–30	101	May 25–29	98
	Sugar beet	May 25–Jun 10	128	May 13–14	131	May 14–29	132	May 05–14	125

Notes:
1. *Soum* is a subprovincial administrative unit in Mongolia, which is equivalent to a district.
2. Data are based on the lower development threshold (presented in Table 20) and 10-year climate data (2008–2017).
3. Growth length is expressed in number of days.

Source: Mongolia's National Agency for Meteorology and Environmental Monitoring.

2.3.2.3 From Whom?

The vegetable farming season in Mongolia is relatively short due to climatic conditions and geographic constraints. Therefore, Mongolians rely on imported vegetables, especially uncommon types, throughout the year.

The market availability of commonly grown vegetables is summarized in Table 22. Peak availability of all vegetables commences right after the new harvest, from late August until the end of December, which covers only a third of a year. The end of the winter and spring seasons sees a reduced supply of Mongolian-produced vegetables in the market. Perishable and/or fresh vegetables such as broccoli, cucumber, lettuce, peas, pepper, snap beans, and tomato are least available, while some root crops, onions, and potatoes are available for about 8–10 months of the year.

Overall, this indicates a poorly developed mechanization and infrastructure for vegetable farming activities throughout the country. The lack of well-developed storage facilities and transportation systems for marketing causes poor supply compared to demand.

Table 22: Market Availability of Most and Least Commonly Produced Vegetables in Mongolia

Item		Jan	Feb	Mar	Apr	May	Jun	Jul	Aug	Sep	Oct	Nov	Dec
Onion	Most									orange	orange		
	Meduim	green	green	green					green	green		green	green
	Least				yellow	yellow	yellow	yellow					
Carrot	Most	orange									orange	orange	orange
	Meduim		green	green	green				green				
	Least					yellow	yellow	yellow					
Potato	Most									orange	orange	orange	orange
	Meduim	green	green	green				green	green				
	Least				yellow	yellow							
Beet and turnip	Most									orange	orange	orange	orange
	Meduim	green	green	green					green				
	Least				yellow	yellow	yellow	yellow					
Tomato	Most									orange	orange		
	Meduim								green				green
	Least	yellow	yellow	yellow	yellow	yellow	yellow	yellow					
Pepper	Most									orange	orange		
	Meduim								green				green
	Least	yellow	yellow	yellow	yellow	yellow	yellow	yellow					
Cucumber	Most									orange	orange		
	Meduim								green			green	green
	Least	yellow	yellow	yellow	yellow	yellow	yellow	yellow					
Strawberry	Most										orange		
	Meduim								green	green			green
	Least	yellow	yellow	yellow	yellow	yellow	yellow	yellow					
Broccoli	Most									orange	orange		
	Meduim								green				green
	Least	yellow	yellow	yellow	yellow	yellow	yellow	yellow					
Lettuce	Most									orange	orange		
	Meduim								green				green
	Least	yellow	yellow	yellow	yellow	yellow	yellow	yellow					
Pea	Most									orange	orange		
	Meduim								green				
	Least	yellow	yellow	yellow	yellow	yellow	yellow	yellow					
Beans, snap	Most									orange	orange		
	Meduim								green			green	green
	Least	yellow	yellow	yellow	yellow	yellow	yellow	yellow					

orange = high availability,   yellow = medium availability,   green = low availability.

Source: Team analysis using field survey data.

Customs data demonstrate that vegetables were imported into Mongolia from various countries during the period 2015–2017 (Table 23).

Table 23: Summary of Customs Import Data of Vegetables, 2015–2017

Year	Potato	Onion and Garlic	Cabbage	Carrot and Turnip	Watermelon
2015	Denmark, France, Germany, Kazakhstan, People's Republic of China, Russian Federation	Canada, Israel, Kazakhstan, Kyrgyz Republic, Macedonia, Netherlands, People's Republic of China, Republic of Korea, Russian Federation	Kazakhstan, People's Republic of China, Republic of Korea, Russian Federation	Kazakhstan, Morocco, People's Republic of China, Republic of Korea, Russian Federation	Argentina, Azerbaijan, Belarus, Belgium, Botswana, Brazil, Chile, Colombia, Czech Republic, Ecuador, Egypt, Germany, Israel, Italy, Japan, Kazakhstan, Kyrgyz Republic, Macedonia, Mexico, Moldova, Morocco, Netherlands, People's Republic of China, Poland, Republic of Korea, Russian Federation, Serbia, South Africa, Turkey
2016	France, Germany, Netherlands, People's Republic of China, Republic of Korea, Russian Federation, United States	India, Italy, Kazakhstan, Kyrgyz Republic, Macedonia, Netherlands, People's Republic of China, Republic of Korea, Russian Federation, Spain, Uzbekistan	France, India, Kazakhstan, Kyrgyz Republic, Netherlands, People's Republic of China, Poland, Republic of Korea, Russian Federation, South Africa, Spain	Belarus, Kazakhstan, Kyrgyz Republic, Morocco, Netherlands, People's Republic of China, Republic of Korea, Russian Federation	Brazil, Costa Rica, Honduras, India, Iran, Kazakhstan, Kyrgyz Republic, Panama, People's Republic of China, Republic of Korea, Russian Federation, Spain, Uzbekistan
2017	France, Germany, People's Republic of China	France, India, Italy, Kazakhstan, Macedonia, Netherlands, People's Republic of China, Republic of Korea, Russian Federation, Spain	France, India, Italy, Kazakhstan, Macedonia, Netherlands, People's Republic of China, Republic of Korea, Russian Federation, Spain	Kazakhstan, Kyrgyz Republic, Netherlands, People's Republic of China, Republic of Korea, Russian Federation	Brazil, Chile, Costa Rica, Ecuador, Kazakhstan, Panama, People's Republic of China, Republic of Korea, Russian Federation, Spain, Viet Nam, Yemen

Source: Customs General Administration of Mongolia.

Vegetable import volumes and values between 2012 and 2017 are shown in Table 24 and Table 25, respectively. Table 26 shows unit prices of vegetables imported into Mongolia in the same period. Local prices were calculated based on official data from the Bank of Mongolia (or MongolBank, the central bank of Mongolia) on mean monthly exchange rates for the respective years.

Table 24: Vegetable Import Volumes, 2012–2017
('000 ton)

Item	2012	2013	2014	2015	2016	2017	CAGR (%)
Potato	3.2	–	5.4	17.1	0.7	0.4	(34)
Tomato	3.5	3.4	4.1	3.9	1.7	0.7	(28)
Onion, garlic	10.5	16.2	19.1	8.6	12.4	17.4	11
Cabbage	34.5	23.1	23.9	24.5	24.6	30.0	(3)
Carrot, turnip	18.5	10.4	9.1	2.3	8.6	9.9	(12)
Cucumber	1.3	3.0	3.0	3.3	1.8	0.7	(12)
Watermelon	5.7	6.4	5.9	5.3	14.7	0.8	(32)
Total, including potato	77.2	62.5	70.5	65.0	64.5	59.9	(5)

– = zero value, ( ) = negative value, CAGR = compound annual growth rate.
Source: Customs Statistics by the Customs General Administration of Mongolia.

Mongolian statistical customs data during 2012–2017 indicate that vegetable imports decreased from 77.2 kt to 59.9 kt (CAGR of –5%). Imports of potato, tomato, and watermelon decreased the most, with potato imports, for instance, decreasing from 3.2 kt in 2012 to 0.4 kt in 2017 (CAGR of –34%). Conversely, onion and garlic imports increased by a CAGR of 11% in the same period.

A similar trend in the total value of vegetables imported between 2012 and 2017 is shown in Table 25. Increases in unit prices of individual vegetables, shown in Table 26, accounted for a smaller decrease in total value of imported vegetables, with an average reduction in CAGR of 2% over the period.

Table 25: Vegetable Import Values, 2012–2017
($'000)

Item	2012	2013	2014	2015	2016	2017	CAGR (%)
Potato	886.1	10.5	1,008.3	3,468.2	215.2	109.9	(34)
Tomato	839.2	942.5	1,137.5	942.1	422.1	192.0	(26)
Onion, garlic	1,861.1	2,781.1	3,584.9	2,227.3	2,714.2	3,694.1	15
Cabbage	5,156.6	3,617.0	4,424.6	4,603.3	4,885.3	5,536.4	1
Carrot, turnip	2,648.6	1,516.2	1,483.5	518.4	1,595.5	1,810.8	(7)
Cucumber	380.6	791.9	825.9	776.6	434.7	169.0	(15)
Watermelon	881.3	950.6	1,017.6	1,015.7	2,123.7	189.4	(26)
Total, including potato	12,653.5	10,609.8	13,482.3	13,551.6	12,390.7	11,701.6	(2)

( ) = negative value, CAGR = compound annual growth rate.
Source: Customs Statistics by the Customs General Administration of Mongolia.

Table 26: Unit Prices of Imported Vegetables, 2012–2017
(MNT per kilogram)

Item	2012	2013	2014	2015	2016	2017	CAGR (%)
Potato	376.4		339.5	399.6	659.7	670.4	12
Tomato	325.9	421.9	504.4	475.9	532.8	669.3	15
Onion, garlic	240.9	261.3	341.2	510.2	469.7	518.0	17
Cabbage	203.2	238.3	336.6	370.1	426.2	450.3	17
Carrot, turnip	194.6	221.9	296.4	444.0	398.1	446.3	18
Cucumber	397.9	401.8	500.5	463.6	518.3	589.1	8
Watermelon	210.2	226.1	313.6	377.5	310.0	577.7	22

CAGR = compound annual growth rate, MNT = Mongolian togrog.

Source: Team analysis using the Mongolian Customs Statistics and the MongolBank currency exchange rates.

2.3.2.4   How Much Do They Cost?

Unit prices of every vegetable in this study increased during 2012–2017 with an average increase in CAGR of 15%. The overall average unit price increase in CAGR of 12% on imported vegetables closely follows the dollar–togrog exchange rate during the same period (Figure 1).

It is important to note that Mongolia imposes a 5% import tax on most imported goods and some are subject to additional seasonal duties. Cabbage, onion, potato, yellow carrot, and yellow turnip are subject to 15% customs duty between 1 August and 1 April. For the remainder of the year, a 5% customs duty applies.

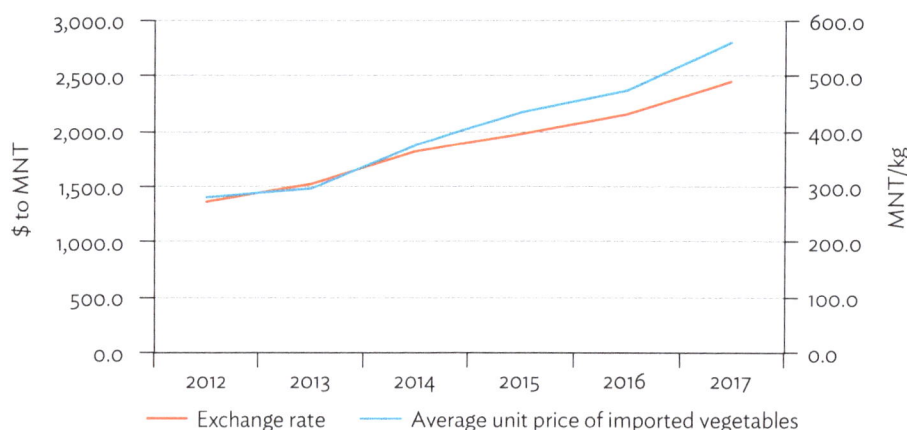

Figure 1: Average Unit Price of Imported Vegetables versus Currency Exchange Rate, 2012–2017

kg = kilogram, MNT = Mongolian togrog.

Source: Team analysis using the Mongolian Customs Statistics and the MongolBank currency exchange rates.

2.4 Drivers of Supply Performance

Some of the underlying reasons for decreased vegetable production in Mongolia include the following:

- *There is a shortage of appropriate storage facilities among households and individual farmers.* As each vegetable type requires different storage parameters, farmers' production is limited by storage capacity.

- *Current open field production is dependent on weather conditions and storage facilities.* Due to limited storage and harvest volumes, most vegetables are sold at MNT500/kg to MNT600/kg to wholesalers and/or retailers. Therefore, the current net profit is not adequate to invest in additional greenhouse infrastructure. There is also a need to train new skilled workers, as the current supply is scarce.

- *There is a shortage of proper and efficient equipment and machinery for seed and seedling sowing, soil cultivation, chemical spraying, watering, and harvesting.* According to the Ministry of Food, Agriculture and Light Industry (MOFALI) statistics, only 10% of vegetable production is mechanized. This indicates that equipment and technological capacity are insufficient. Though regular maintenance is required, the needed parts are not on the market for sale.

- *There are limited opportunities to expand planting areas.* Poor water supply and lack of appropriate irrigation facilities are indicated as among the principal limiting factors.

- *Returns on intensive vegetable production are inadequate.* It would appear that given the current prices of vegetables and the costs of greenhouses, there is insufficient return for producers to invest in, and expand production through, the establishment of new winter greenhouse facilities. This is discussed further in the technical analysis undertaken for this study.

3 VALUE CHAIN ANALYSIS

3.1 Value Chain Map: Marketing Channels, Revenues, Costs, Margins, and Trends

3.1.1 Description of the End-to-End Value Chain for Vegetables in Mongolia

Figure 2 summarizes the generic segments or steps in the vegetable value chain.

Figure 2: Simplified Mapping of Vegetable Value Chain in Mongolia

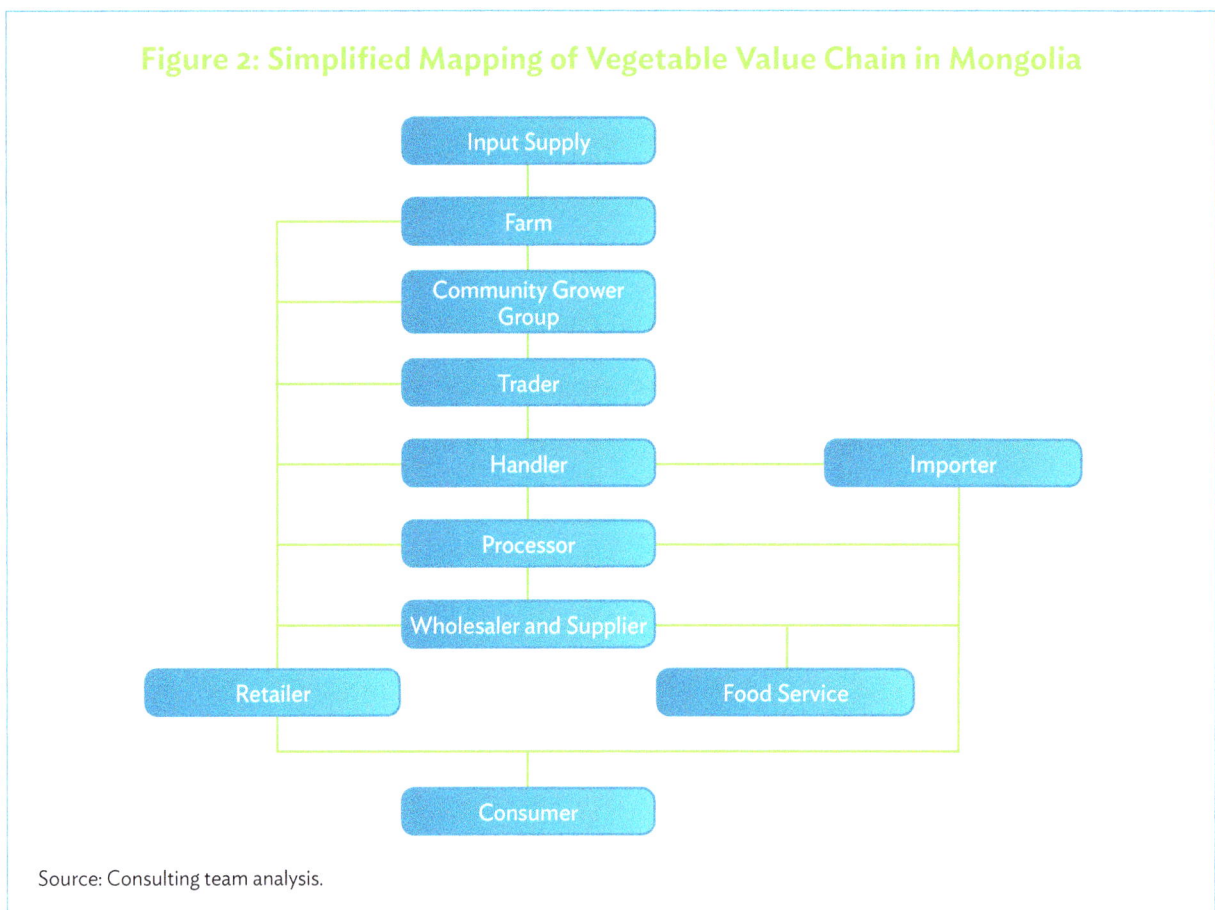

Source: Consulting team analysis.

Figure 3 identifies the dynamics, interrelations, and linkages within the value chain segments, including representative companies and organizations.

Figure 3: Vegetable Value Chain Dynamics in Mongolia

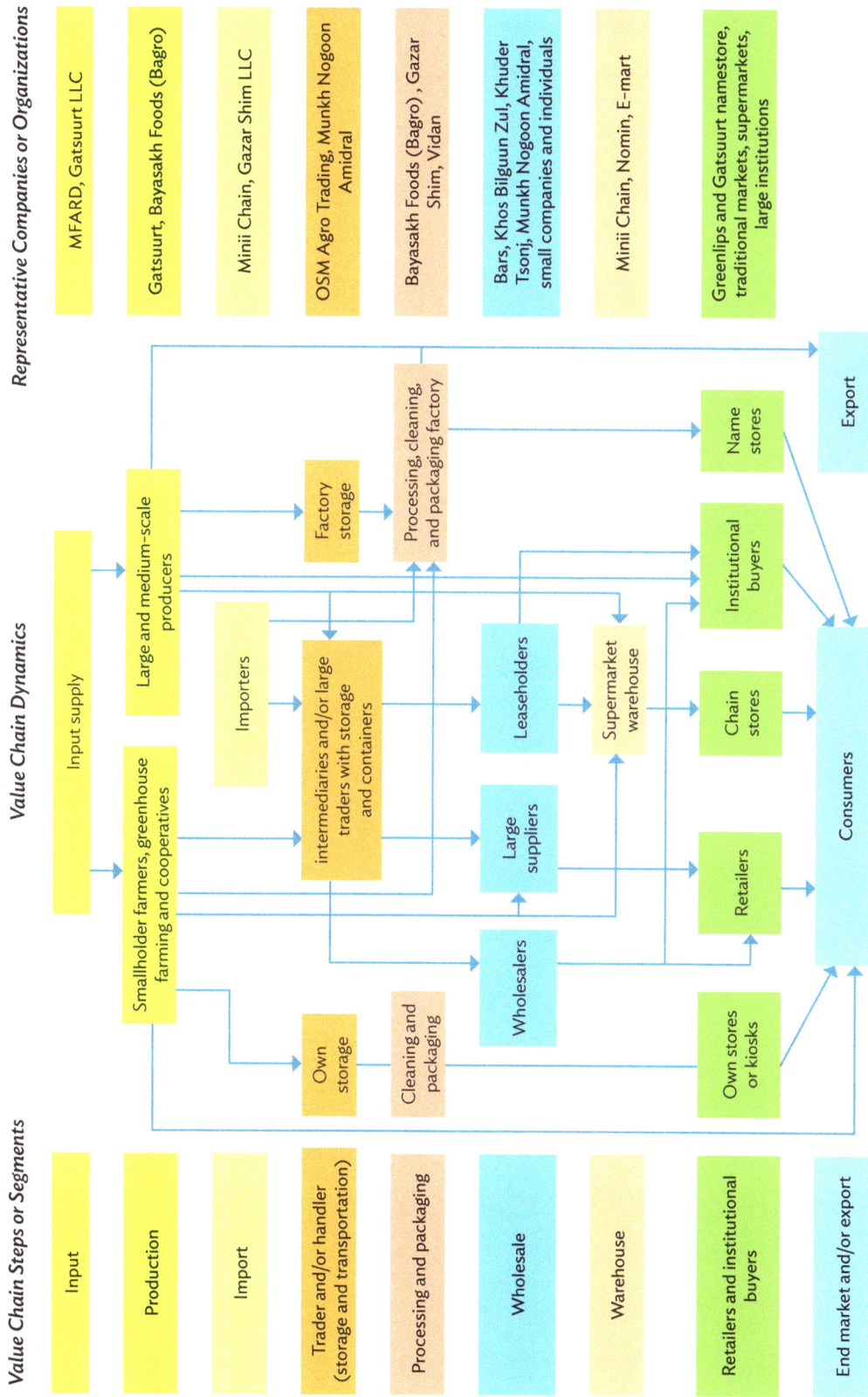

Value Chain Steps or Segments

Value Chain Steps or Segments	Value Chain Dynamics	Representative Companies or Organizations
Input	Input supply	MFARD, Gatsuurt LLC
Production	Large and medium-scale producers; Smallholder farmers, greenhouse farming and cooperatives	Gatsuurt, Bayasakh Foods (Bagro)
Import	Importers	Minii Chain, Gazar Shim LLC
Trader and/or handler (storage and transportation)	Own storage; Factory storage; intermediaries and/or large traders with storage and containers	OSM Agro Trading, Munkh Nogoon Amidral
Processing and packaging	Cleaning and packaging; Processing, cleaning and packaging factory	Bayasakh Foods (Bagro), Gazar Shim, Vidan
Wholesale	Wholesalers; Large suppliers; Leaseholders	Bars, Khos Bilguun Zul, Khuder Tsonj, Munkh Nogoon Amidral, small companies and individuals
Warehouse	Supermarket warehouse	Minii Chain, Nomin, E-mart
Retailers and institutional buyers	Own stores or kiosks; Retailers; Chain stores; Institutional buyers; Name stores	Greenlips and Gatsuurt namestore, traditional markets, supermarkets, large institutions
End market and/or export	Consumers; Export	

LLC =Limited Liability Company, MFARD = Mongolian Farmer Association for Rural Development.
Source: Consulting team analysis.

Sections 3.1.1.1–3.1.1.5 discuss the dynamics of each link in the value chain.

3.1.1.1   Input Supply

The input supply segment includes suppliers of goods (e.g., chemicals, farm equipment, and seeds) and services (e.g., banks, laborers, and leasing companies) for farm vegetable production. Industry-related associations such as the MFARD, the PSARI, and private entities such as Gatsuurt Limited Liability Company (LLC) are included in this segment.

The main seed providers are the MFARD, which is supported by the SDC's VEGI Project and the PSARI. The MFARD operates a vegetable seed fund that supplies quality seeds for the main vegetable crops to farmers in remote areas at wholesale prices. The quality and origin of these seeds are monitored at the national level. The PSARI supplies certified seeds at prices based on their estimated costs of production plus a 20% margin.

Together, the MFARD and the PSARI supply most of the farmers' seed requirements for some major vegetables, such as potatoes. However, almost all seeds for vegetables such as garlic, leafy greens, and onions are imported. Farmers buy seeds directly from the MFARD branches and the PSARI, as well as from traders and seed retailers. The MFARD *aimag* branches serve as seed retailers and distributors to small-scale farmers and association members. The MFARD and the PSARI certify their seeds. Other traders claim to sell MFARD or PSARI seeds, but these claims are not verified.

In 2015, licensed vegetable seed producers from the MFARD branch in Uvs *aimag* supplied about 50%–60% of seed demand for the main vegetable crops, such as beetroot, carrots, and turnips; in 2016, that figure reached 80%. In the 2016 planting season alone, the vegetable seed bank at the MFARD distributed an estimated 4,500 kg of vegetable seeds to the MFARD branches in 17 *aimags* and two seed retailers. A total of 53 seed orders were received, and available seeds were equitably distributed.

Production. The Mongolian vegetable industry consists of three major production sectors and sources of supply: (i) smallholder and greenhouse farmers and cooperatives, (ii) large and medium-scale producers, and (iii) importers.

According to MOFALI, about 35,000 households and 480 cooperatives and companies produce fruit and vegetables. Moreover, around 16,000 smallholder farmers (<3.0 ha/farmer) and 43,200 households (<0.1 ha/household) are engaged in potato and vegetable farming and production. They accounted for 50% (14,800 ha) of the total potato and vegetable plantation area, producing 72% of the nation's potatoes and 64% of its vegetables in 2016. Data from the MOFALI and the National Statistical Office (NSO) of Mongolia indicate that, within the project implementing *soums*, 16 companies and 430 household farmers in Bornuur, 29 companies and 374 household farmers in Orkhon, 13 companies and 163 household farmers in Ulaangom, and 2 companies and 237 household farmers in Yeruu are active in potato and vegetable growing businesses.

Polyvinyl cold-frame summer greenhouses are commonly used by farmers in Mongolia. These types of greenhouses extend the growing season by at least 2 months and allow farmers to harvest 2 months earlier on average. Experienced growers tend to invest in these types of greenhouses, as they can safely grow specialty crops such as long cucumber, leafy vegetables, sweet pepper, tomato, and zucchini that normally have higher market value and demand. According to the Greenhouse Vegetable Growers Federation, demand for fresh vegetables grown in greenhouses is increasing every year. Market prices in spring and early summer are much more competitive (almost 3–4 times higher than the August–September prices). Therefore, farmers attempt to produce these crops in greenhouses as early as possible. The average size of summer greenhouses is 120 square meters (m^2) and 240 m^2. During visits to the field sites, the consulting team observed that an average household grower possesses one of these size greenhouses. Winter greenhouses or year-round greenhouses are used by a few farmers, especially in the area surrounding Ulaanbaatar. Winter greenhouses require adequate heating, ventilation, and irrigation infrastructure, which makes the cost of construction challenging for individual growers.

Large and medium-scale producers (there are 60 large farms on >30 ha and 1,250 medium-sized farms on 3–30 ha) account for the rest of the domestic production. One representative large vegetable producer with its own supply and value chain is Gatsuurt LLC. Gatsuurt plants and harvests 150 different types of vegetables, including 25 types of potato, on 454 ha of land. It sells its produce through seven of its own brand name stores in Ulaanbaatar and 3,000 contracted large and small sales points nationwide.

Market mapping analysis demonstrates a 70% self-sufficiency rate, on average, for domestic potato and vegetable production as of 2017. This confirms that 30% of potato and vegetables consumed in Mongolia is being imported from foreign markets.

3.1.1.2   Trader and Handler

Most smallholder farmers and importers sell their products to intermediary traders as quickly as possible after harvesting or importing to prevent the loss of perishable vegetables.[13] In most cases, the intermediaries also provide transportation and storage of vegetables. By contrast, many large and medium-sized producers have their own handling facilities. During consultations, one key informant stated that the trader segment is relatively concentrated, with around 10 large players having well-established operations alongside numerous smaller-scale traders and handlers.

3.1.1.3   Processing

Processing technologies range from simple cleaning and packaging at large producers, vegetable stalls, supermarkets, and markets to jar-packaged pickled products and processed mixed salads produced at dedicated factories. During field research, a representative from the private sector shared that the domestic vegetable processing market has expanded by 5% in the last 5 years and that this trend is likely to continue. Currently, the domestic vegetable processing industry comprises four main participants: Gazar Shim, Bagro, Vidan, and Shimt Gazar. External competition is strong, and imported jar-packaged pickled vegetables are readily available.

---

[13]   Swiss Agency for Development and Cooperation (SDC). 2018. *Annual Report 2017.* Ulaanbaatar.

3.1.1.4   Wholesale

The wholesale segment comprises large suppliers, leaseholders, and wholesalers that buy in bulk from traders or intermediaries and sell to retailers and institutional buyers or directly to consumers. The main vegetable wholesale point is the Bars outdoor and indoor market, the main branch of which is located in central Ulaanbaatar, close to the railroad and major roads. District markets, such as Amgalan, Bayanzurkh, Kharhorin, and Khuchit Shonkhor, also serve as wholesale vegetable hubs in the city.

3.1.1.5   Retailers and Institutional Buyers

Retailers, supermarkets, markets, and institutional buyers source their supplies from wholesalers, large suppliers, and leaseholders at wholesale points. Large institutional buyers and large retail chain buyers collaborate with large vegetable suppliers to obtain consistent supply throughout the year of products that meet their standard. Large and medium-sized producers like Gatsuurt LLC recently introduced pioneering agricultural projects that skip the intermediaries and provide products directly to the retailers, institutional buyers, and consumers through brand name stores. Additionally, some greenhouse farmers have developed semiautonomous supply and value chains. They have their own storage and warehouse facilities and sell products directly to consumers through their own shops or rented stalls at markets, without the involvement of traders or wholesalers.

3.2   Competitive Market Landscape: Shares of Domestic Suppliers, Imports, Nature of Competition, and Trends

3.2.1   Who Are the Major Suppliers of Promising Crops?

Agricultural companies, including larger crop farming entities; other organizations and enterprises such as schools, restaurants, and supermarkets; and smallholder farmers all contribute to the supply of promising crops. Smallholder vegetable growers play a major role in the cultivation of potatoes and vegetables. In 2016, as shown in Table 27 and Figure 4, they contributed 119.1 kt (72% of total production) of potatoes and 76.8 kt (64% of total production) of vegetables, nationally. Agricultural companies, including larger crop farming entities, and other organizations and enterprises such as schools, restaurants, and supermarkets contributed 28% of potatoes and 15% of vegetables. Only about 0.03% of the entire potato supply chain by volume was imported, whereas imports constituted about 21% of the total vegetable market.

Table 27: Production of Potato and Vegetable Suppliers, 2016
(ton)

Item	Harvest of Smallholders	Harvest of Agricultural Companies	Total Imported	Nationwide Consumption
Potato	119,054.5	46,275.0	49.7	165,379.2
Vegetables	76,840.4	17,606.8	25,744.2	120,191.4

Source: National Statistical Office of Mongolia.

The data show that Mongolia's major suppliers of potatoes are smallholder growers and larger agricultural companies. In the case of vegetables, major suppliers are smallholder growers, agricultural companies, and some enterprises that undertake importing activities.

Figure 4: Structure of Potato and Vegetable Supply Chain, 2016

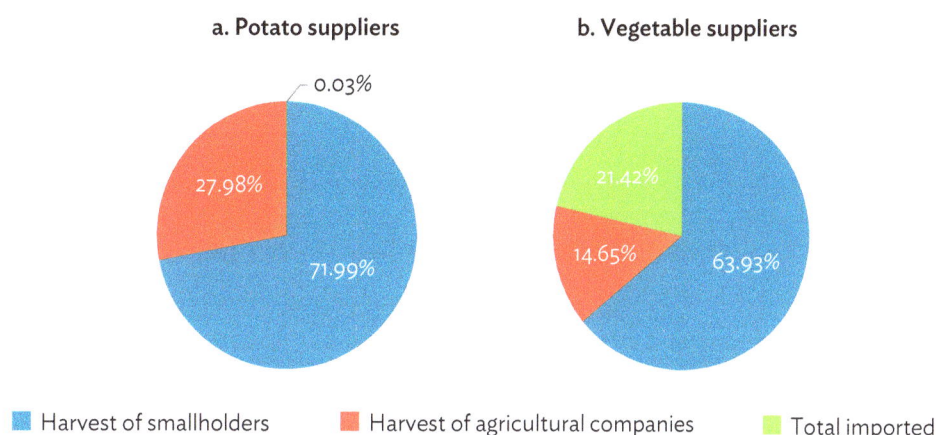

a. Potato suppliers   **b. Vegetable suppliers**

a. Potato suppliers: 0.03%, 27.98%, 71.99%

b. Vegetable suppliers: 21.42%, 14.65%, 63.93%

■ Harvest of smallholders   ■ Harvest of agricultural companies   ■ Total imported

Source: National Statistical Office of Mongolia.

The bulk of total national yields of smallholder vegetable growers comes from the four project *aimags* (Table 28).

Table 28: Smallholder Vegetable Growers' Contributions to Potato and Vegetable Production, 2016

	Potato			Vegetables		
Aimag	Total Yield (ton)	Yield of Smallholder (ton)	% in Total Yield	Total Yield (ton)	Yield of Smallholder (ton)	% in Total Yield
Nationwide	165,329.5	119,054.5	72.01	94,447.2	76,840.4	81.36
Uvs	3,191.5	2,633.9	82.53	3,404.7	2,992.3	87.89
Darkhan-Uul	7,420.5	5,399.5	72.76	14,358.8	12,669.6	88.24
Selenge	42,487.6	23,004.0	54.14	32,715.6	24,808.6	75.83
Tuv	64,696.6	49,905.0	77.14	8,074.4	6,252.2	77.43

Note: *Aimag* refers to the provincial administrative unit in Mongolia.
Source: National Statistical Office of Mongolia.

The NSO's data suggest intermediary suppliers could play an important role in potato and vegetable supply chains. In 2015, these suppliers spent MNT435.8 billion on domestic production from the crop-farming sector. As shown in Figure 5, households, as end users, were the largest consumer, spending about 40% (MNT318.4 billion), followed by animal farming-related users (27%), and food and beverage manufacturers (16%).

The most important suppliers of promising vegetables are smallholder growers located near larger cities such as Darkhan, Erdenet, and Ulaanbaatar. Majority of these vegetables—root crops, cruciferous, and allium types—are cultivated in open fields, as shown in Table 3. A smaller portion of vegetables is grown in closed-cultivation areas such as in summer and in 3-season or 4-season greenhouses. Cucumbers, leafy green vegetables, sweet peppers, and tomatoes are supplied by farmers who mostly

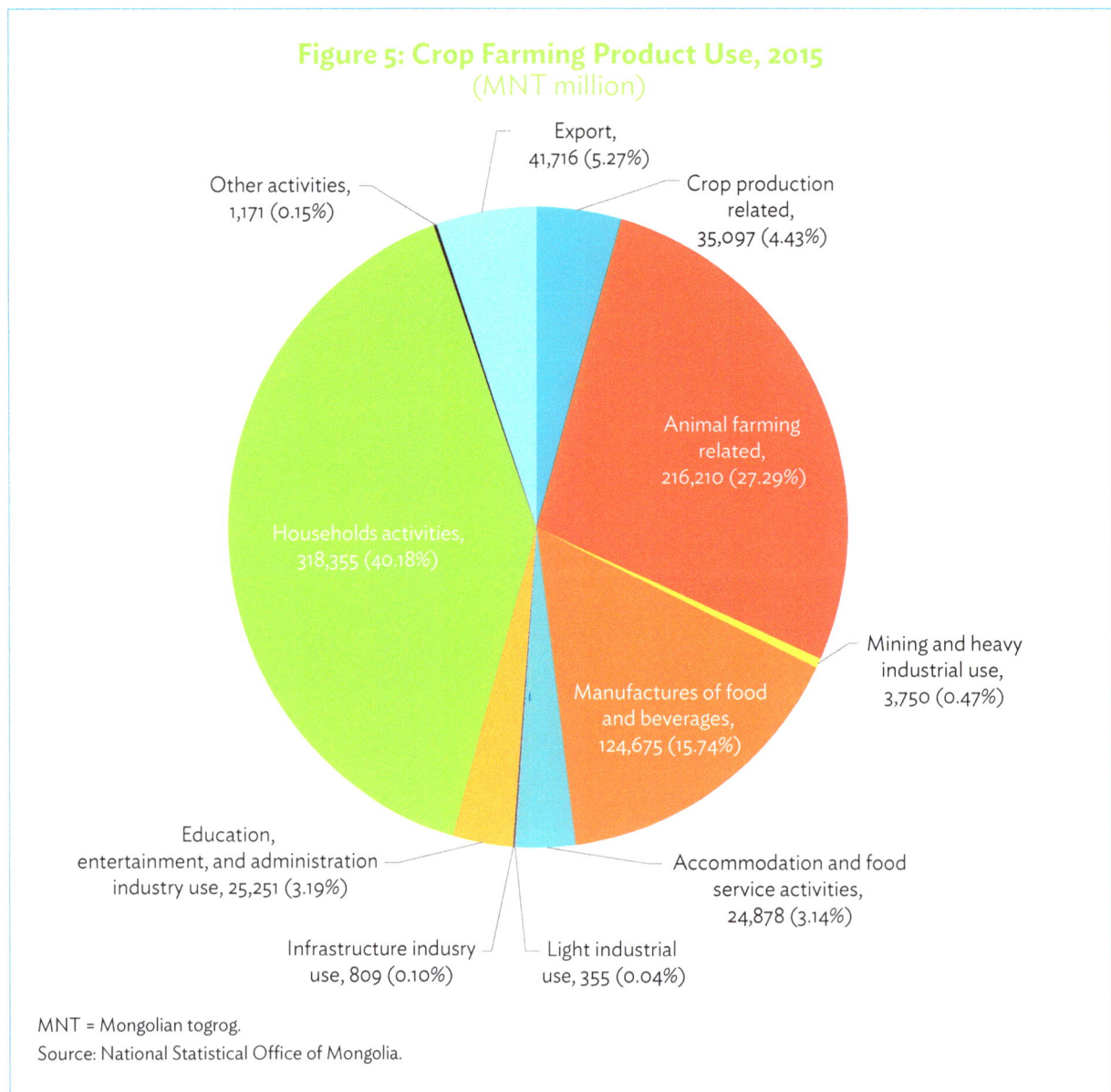

Figure 5: Crop Farming Product Use, 2015
(MNT million)

Export, 41,716 (5.27%)

Crop production related, 35,097 (4.43%)

Other activities, 1,171 (0.15%)

Animal farming related, 216,210 (27.29%)

Households activities, 318,355 (40.18%)

Mining and heavy industrial use, 3,750 (0.47%)

Manufactures of food and beverages, 124,675 (15.74%)

Education, entertainment, and administration industry use, 25,251 (3.19%)

Accommodation and food service activities, 24,878 (3.14%)

Infrastructure indusry use, 809 (0.10%)

Light industrial use, 355 (0.04%)

MNT = Mongolian togrog.
Source: National Statistical Office of Mongolia.

use greenhouse facilities near the Ulaanbaatar area. Due to climate conditions, winter greenhouse (4-season) technologies have not been widely adopted. Therefore, most greenhouse-grown vegetables are imported.

In 2017, about 150 companies were involved in potato and vegetable import businesses (as depicted in Table 29 as number of import cases), with 20 companies importing potatoes and 130 companies importing vegetables. Total expenditure on potato imports was $0.21 million, while vegetable imports reached $15.60 million.

Table 29: Number of Mongolian-Based Companies Involved in Potato and Vegetable Imports, 2017

	Cases of Import							Number of Import	Amount (ton)	Expense ($)
Item	<10	11–50	51–200	201–500	501–1,000	1,001–2,000	<2,001			
Potato	17	3	0	0	0	0	0	123	1,145	211,866
Vegetables	73	16	14	10	9	6	2	25,930	75,334	15,597,124

Source: Customs General Administration of Mongolia.

3.2.2 Analysis of Product Prices in Ulaanbaatar Markets

Data for this project has been collected from several sources, including official statistics, a pilot survey of sales outlets, a pilot survey of farmers, and interviews with sector representatives during structured investigations. The results of this analysis are included in the following discussion of price margins along the identified value chains.

3.2.3 Distribution of Margins Across Segments of Relevant Value Chains

Five main potato and vegetable value chains have been identified, as summarized in Table 30.

Table 30: Main Value Chains for Potatoes and Vegetables in Mongolia

Main Value Chains Identified	
Value chain 1	Smallholder farmers and/or individual growers—traders and/or large suppliers—wholesalers—markets and/or supermarkets (retailers)—consumers
Value chain 2	Large and/or medium-scale farmers—name stores, supermarkets, or other retail points—consumers
Value chain 3	Importers—traders and/or large suppliers—wholesalers—markets and/or supermarkets (retailers)—consumers
Value chain 4	Smallholder farmers and/or individual growers or importers—processing factories—markets and/or supermarkets (retailers)—consumers
Value chain 5	Smallholder farmers and/or individual growers or large and/or medium-scale farmers—large retailer "C"—consumers (direct procurement model)

Note: Large retailer "C" refers to a fairly new supermarket entrant who procures vegetables directly from farmers, subject to specified standards and norms.

Source: Consulting team analysis.

To analyze product prices and price margins across the identified value chain segments, five types of vegetables have been selected due to data availability and consistency: cabbage, carrot, onion, potato, and turnip.

To assess farm gate prices, the consulting team held phone interviews with several farmers. Trader and large supplier prices were obtained via phone and in-person interviews with relevant industry players. Wholesale vegetable prices at wholesale markets and individual retailers (traditional markets and supermarkets) were obtained from Ulaanbaatar statistics (2015–2017). Average annual retail prices have been calculated based on monthly records.

3.2.3.1   Value Chain 1: Smallholder Farmers and/or Individual Growers—Traders and/or Large Suppliers—Wholesalers— Markets and/or Supermarkets (Retail)— Consumers

Table 31 shows product prices (expressed in MNT per kg) and price margins (total percentage increase and percentage increase at each value chain step and/or stage) across the value chain segments identified in value chain 1.

This value chain is the most common among smallholder farmers in Mongolia. According to both the literature reviewed and interviews with farmers, most smallholder farmers choose to sell products to traders or intermediaries. Traders arrive at farms in their own vehicles and purchase vegetables in exchange for cash at farm gate prices, which vary annually depending on supply and other factors.

The analysis in this section shows the price margins and, hence, the amounts added to prices by intermediaries and other participants as vegetables move along the value chain. The amounts added are described in the commentary following the value chain tables, with price data for each chain.

Identifying the gross margin (defined as revenue minus variable costs) entails having data on value chain participants' costs. These data were not provided, except through the pilot farm surveys conducted in the four project *soums*. Transport costs for participants are identified in relation to the changes in the value chain (and, hence, returns arising from those changes), when these are estimated for each of the value chain models in sections 3.2.3.1—3.2.3.5.

Regarding value chain 1:

- ■ Traders and/or intermediaries generally possess large storage facilities and/or containers, and they supply wholesalers and institutional buyers in large quantities. A price margin of 32%–50% was added to cabbage, carrot, and potato by traders when sold to large suppliers. In the case of turnips, a 192% increase on farm gate prices can be observed. On average, selected vegetable prices show a 61% increase.

- ■ Wholesalers in Mongolia purchase vegetables from traders and/or intermediaries. For the five vegetables studied, an average of 82% is added to the traders and/or large suppliers' prices. This is a 223% price increase on farm gate prices.

Table 31: Value Chain 1—Farm Gate to Traders and/or Large Suppliers to Wholesalers to Markets and/or Supermarkets
(MNT per kilogram)

Vegetable	Farm Gate to Trader/Intermediaries[a]			Large Supplier[b]			Wholesaler (Bars)[c]			Traditional Market[c]			Supermarket Store[c]		
	Min	Max	Ave	Min	Max	Ave	Min	Max	Ave	Min	Max	Ave	Min	Max	Ave
Potato	300	600	450	500	700	600	842		842	900	1,083	992	891	1,217	1,054
% increase						133%			187%			220%			234%
% increase in each stage						33%			54%			33%			14%
Carrot	500		500	500	1,000	750	1,117		1,117	1,200	1,450	1,325	1,136	1,532	1,334
% increase						150%			223%			265%			267%
% increase in each stage						50%			73%			42%			2%
Cabbage	550	700	625	800	850	825	1,508		1,508	1,408	1,758	1,583	1,725	2,075	1,900
% increase						132%			241%			253%			304%
% increase in each stage						32%			209%			44%			51%
Turnip	400	800	600	1,000	2,500	1,750	1,933		1,933	1,650	2,308	1,979	1,999	2,056	2,028
% increase						292%			322%			330%			338%
% increase in each stage						192%			31%			8%			8%
Onion	800	1,000	900	800	1,000	900	1,275		1,275	1,325	1,667	1,496	1,318	1,695	1,507
% increase						100%			142%			166%			167%
% increase in each stage						0%			42%			25%			1%
Overall average % increase						161%			223%			247%			262%
Overall average % increase in each stage						61%			82%			30%			15%

Ave = average, Max = maximum, Min = minimum, MNT = Mongolian togrog.

a Farm gate prices were obtained from a member of the Farmer's Association in Selenge aimag (Naraa, 99490078).
b Munkh Nogoon Amidral produces common and specialty vegetables. Moreover, this company acts as a intermediaries that collects vegetables from farmers in Selenge aimag; and markets them to various retailers, including large supermarkets, e.g., Nomin and Good Price. For this service, the company charges 10% from total sales of the vegetables. Figures illustrated in the above table indicate values from 2017.
c Bar (wholesaler), traditional market, retailer, and supermarket prices have been extracted from the Ulaanbaatar Statistics (found in Sheet d, Analysis of Product Prices).

Source: Consulting team analysis.

- Traditional retailers, known as *zakh* (market), and small and medium-sized shops buy vegetables from large supplier containers, if they have access, or in most cases, from wholesalers. At this stage, approximately 30% is added to the wholesale prices.

- Supermarkets procure vegetables through various channels, according to interviews with various supermarket procurement managers. Some buy vegetables from large suppliers or leaseholders and small individual producers, while some import vegetables themselves. The average price difference compared to the traditional retail market is around 15%. However, compared to the farm gate prices, the supermarket value is increased by 262%, on average. Similarly, the overall price increases of potato and carrot ranged between 234% and 267%. Cabbage and turnip prices increased the most, from 304% to 338%. Onion had the least percentage increase of 167%.

3.2.3.2   Value Chain 2: Large and/or Medium-Scale Farmers—Name Stores, Supermarkets, or Other Retail Points—Consumers

Table 32 illustrates the second value chain: a large or medium-scale farmer or producer that sells its products through its own brand name stores or other large supermarkets.

Regarding value chain 2:

- This value chain is noteworthy because the large producer is able to skip the trader and/or intermediary stage and sell vegetables to end-consumers at an earlier stage of the value chain.

- The farmers' gate prices to traders are shown in the second column of Table 32. They provide a comparison between the farmers' prices to intermediary traders versus the large producer's brand name store retail prices shown in the third column. Brand name store prices of producer and/or retailer "A" are 35% higher than the farm gate prices on average. Supermarket prices at retailers "B" and "C" show an increase of 85%–101%, as compared to brand name store prices of large producer and/or retailer "A".

- Some vegetable prices increased significantly when producer A's products were sold through retailer B's wholesale stores (fourth column). For instance, potatoes were sold at 277% higher than in its own brand name store price, while carrot prices increased by 176%, and onion prices by 150%.

Table 32: Value Chain 2—Large and/or Medium-Scale Farmers to Name Stores, Supermarkets, or Other Retail Points to Consumers
(MNT per kilogram)

Vegetable	Farm Gate to Trader/ Intermediaries			Producer/Retailer "A" Name Store Price			Producer "A" Product Price at Retailer "B" Wholesale Store			Producer "A" Product Price at Retailer "C" Supermarket (Consumer)		
	Min	Max	Ave	Min	Max	Ave	Min	Max	Ave	Min	Max	Ave
Potato	300	600	450	650	650	650	1,799	1,799	1,799	1,100	1,100	1,100
% increase			69%			100%			277%			169%
% increase in each stage			(31%)						177%			69%
Carrot	500		500	850		850	1,499		1,499	1,700		1,700
% increase			59%			100%			176%			200%
% increase in each stage			(41%)						76%			100%
Cabbage	550	700	625	1250		1,250	–	–		–	–	
% increase			50%			100%						
% increase in each stage			(50%)									
Turnip	400	800	600	950		950	–			–		
% increase			63%			100%						
% increase in each stage			(37%)									
Onion	800	1,000	900	1,100		1,100	1,649		1,649	–		
% increase						100%			150%			
% increase in each stage									50%			
Overall average % increase									201%			185%
Overall average % increase in each stage									101%			85%

( ) = negative value, – = no data, Ave = average, Max = maximum, Min = minimum, MNT = Mongolian togrog.

Notes:

1. Gatsuurt LLC harvests, stores, transports, cleans, packs, markets, and sells, basically providing the whole value chain.
2. Gatsuurt vegetable prices obtained from the store via phone call. Nomin and E-mart's prices were extracted from the project consulting team's March 2018 pilot study.

Source: Consulting team analysis.

3.2.3.3   Value Chain 3: Importers—Traders and/or Large Suppliers—Wholesalers—Markets and/or Supermarkets (Retailers)—Consumers

The third value chain in Table 33 shows how imported vegetables reach consumers. Large suppliers or intermediaries play a significant role in this value chain, capitalizing on their comparative advantage of owning large volume storage facilities and warehouses.

Regarding value chain 3:

- Imported vegetables are bulk purchased by traders and/or large suppliers who add an average of 85% to the import prices. Percentage increases vary considerably depending on the type of vegetable. For instance, increases in the prices of cabbage (83%), carrots (169%), and onions (69%) were much higher, as compared to the prices of potatoes (19%).

- At the wholesaler stage, the average price increase equals 21%, while traditional markets increase prices by 104%. Here again, price increases vary considerably depending on the type of vegetable.

- Commonly imported vegetables are sold mainly through traditional markets rather than through large supermarket chains. Interviews with large suppliers suggested that food service industry players and some large institutional buyers tend to purchase imported vegetables, especially those originating from the People's Republic of China due to seemingly lower prices.

3.2.3.4   Value Chain 4: Smallholder Farmers and/or Individual Growers or Importers—Processing Factories—Markets and/or Supermarkets (Retailers)—Consumers

Vegetable procurement for processing companies is the fourth identified value chain (Table 34).

Regarding value chain 4:

- Our research indicates that some vegetables were purchased by processing companies at lower prices than the farm gate prices. Specifically, carrots were procured at 94% and turnips at 49% below farm gate prices, while onions were seemingly purchased at a higher price (222%).

- The most common processed vegetables are carrots, cucumbers, and turnips, which are pickled, mixed, and packaged mostly in glass jars. Retail prices of processed products are shown in Table 34 (different volumes, packaging, and processing methods should be taken into account; thus, the figures provided are not directly comparable).

Table 33: Value Chain 3—Importers to Traders and/or Large Suppliers to Wholesalers to Markets and/or Supermarkets (Retailers) to Consumers
(MNT per kilogram)

Vegetable	Import Unit Price (Mongolian Customs Data)			Large Supplier/ Intermediaries			Consumer					
							Bars Group			Traditional Market/ Retailer		
	Min	Max	Ave	Min	Max	Ave	Min	Max	Ave	Min	Max	Ave
Potato	670		670	700	900	800	750	750	750			
% increase			100%			119%			94%			
% increase in each stage						19%			(26%)			
Carrot	446		446	1,100	1,300	1,200	1,300	1,500	1,400			
% increase			100%			269%			314%			
% increase in each stage						169%			45%			
Cabbage	450		450	800	850	825	1,000		1,000	1,500		1,500
% increase			100%			183%			222%			333%
% increase in each stage						83%			39%			111%
Turnip	446		446	–			–			–		
% increase			100%									
% increase in each stage												
Onion	518		518	850	900	875	1,000		1,000	1,500		1,500
% increase			100%			169%			193%			290%
% increase in each stage						69%			24%			97%
Overall average % increase						185%			206%			311%
Overall average % increase in each stage						85%			21%			104%

( ) = negative value, – = no data, Ave = average, Max = maximum, Min = minimum, MNT = Mongolian togrog.

Notes:

1. Wholesale prices of imported from the People's Republic of China have been obtained from a retailer (Urnaa, 88661656), who regularly purchases vegetables from large suppliers (April 2018).
2. Prices for Bars have been obtained from the project team's March 2018 pilot study.

Source: Consulting team analysis.

Table 34: Value Chain 4—Smallholder Farmers and/or Individual Growers or Importers to Processing Factories to Markets and/or Supermarkets (Retailers) to Consumers
(MNT per kilogram)

Vegetable	Farm Gate to Trader/ Intermediaries			Procurement Cost of Processing Company			Consumer — Supermarket Price (500–550 ml jar)			Supermarket Price (720 ml jar)			Supermarket Price (2,550 ml jar)		
	Min	Max	Ave	Min	Max	Ave	Min	Max	Ave	Min	Max	Ave	Min	Max	Ave
Potato	300	600	450				–			–			–		
% increase			100%												
% increase in each stage															
Carrot	500		500	470		470	2,190	3,200	2,695						
% increase			100%			94%			539%						
% increase in each stage									445%						
Cabbage	550	700	625	724		724									
% increase			100%			116%									
% increase in each stage															
Turnip	400	800	600	294		294	2,280	–	2,280	3,250	–	3,250			
% increase			100%			49%			380%			542%			
% increase in each stage									331%						
Onion	800	1,000	900	2,000		2,000	–			–			–		
% increase			100%			222%									
% increase in each stage															
Cucumber				674		674				3,750	5,600	4,675	10,420		10,420
% increase						100%						694%			1546%
% increase in each stage												594%			1446%
Overall average % increase						116%			460%			618%			1546%
Overall average % increase in each stage									388%			594%			1446%

Ave = average, – = no data, Max = maximum, Min = minimum, ml = milliliter, MNT = Mongolian togrog.

Notes:

1. Vegetable procurement costs by processing factories were obtained from GBT Trading LLC (2017 data).
2. Shelf prices for jar-packaged, ready-made vegetable products (mostly pickles and salads) were obtained from Home Plaza and Good Price supermarket visits in April 2018.
3. Carrot prices were based on prices of mixed salad with primarily carrot content.

Source: Consulting team analysis.

3.2.3.5   Value Chain 5: Smallholder Farmers and/or Individual Growers or Large and/or Medium-Scale Farmers—Large Retailer "C"—Consumers (Direct Procurement Model)

Recently, larger supermarkets have begun implementing more innovative vegetable procurement methods. For instance, large retailer "C", a fairly new supermarket entrant, has started to procure vegetables directly from farmers, subject to fulfillment of certain standards and norms (Table 35).

Table 35: Value Chain 5—Smallholder Farmers and/or Individual Growers or Large and/or Medium-Scale Farmers to Large Retailer "C" to Consumers
(MNT per kilogram)

Vegetable	Farm Gate to Trader and/or Intermediaries			Farmer's Price (calculated)			Large Retailer "C" Price from March 2018 Pilot Study			
	Min	Max	Ave	Min	Max	Ave	Min	Max	Ave	
Potato	300	600	**450**	802	1,240	**1,021**	960	1,550	**1,255**	
% increase						**227%**	120%	125%	**122%**	
% increase in each stage										
Carrot	500		**500**	1,044	1,360	**1,202**	1,250	1,700	**1,475**	
% increase						**240%**	120%	125%	**122%**	
% increase in each stage										
Cabbage	550	700	**625**	2,071	1,984	**2,027**	2,480		**2,480**	Consumer
% increase						**324%**	120%	125%	**122%**	
% increase in each stage										
Turnip	400	800	**600**	2,422	2,320	**2,371**	2,900		**2,900**	
% increase						**395%**	120%	125%	**122%**	
% increase in each stage										
Onion	800	1000	**900**	1,319	1,264	**1,292**	1,580		**1,580**	
% increase						**144%**	120%	125%	**122%**	
% increase in each stage										
Overall average % increase						**266%**	**120%**	**125%**	**122%**	
Overall average % increase in each stage							**20%**	**25%**	**22%**	

Ave = average, Max = maximum, Min = minimum, MNT = Mongolian togrog.

Note: Based on interview with E-mart chief operating officer, Mr. Mashbat: "E-Mart's system of directly purchasing from farmers has led to its retail prices falling by 20%–25%."

Source: Consulting team analysis.

Regarding value chain 5:

■ This is a "win-win" model that enables both the seller and the buyer to benefit by eliminating intermediary-associated costs. Although the procurement costs were not readily available, the consulting team calculated the above prices based on an interview with an official representing retailer C.

■ If the above calculations are correct, then it can be seen that this model benefits farmers the most. Compared to farm gate prices, it offers price increases of 144%–395%, depending on the type of vegetable. The average increase in prices equals 266%.

3.3   Strengths and Weaknesses of Value Chains in Meeting Market Needs for Volume, Price, and Quality

3.3.1   Discussions of Key Results

The most common route for vegetables to pass along the value chain is from farmers, importers, and large producers to intermediaries. Intermediaries then sell the vegetables to wholesalers at higher prices. Retailers and institutional buyers purchase supplies from wholesalers. Finally, end-consumers buy vegetables from retailers, chain stores, institutional buyers, and name stores.

The difference in the value chain margin for smallholder farmers between selling vegetables to an intermediary and selling directly to retailers and institutional buyers is significant. For instance, the average farm gate price for potato was MNT450, while in the direct procurement model, value chain 5, the estimated average farmer's price was MNT1,021. This represents a 127% increase in price with a margin of MNT571. There are, however, some disincentives for farmers to sell directly to retailers. For instance, retailers are closer to consumers and, therefore, have much more detailed information on market demand than farmers (and other intermediaries). Retailers, thereby, set specifications in response to consumer demand for quality, which not all farmers can meet.

Moreover, most retailers purchase vegetables on a consignment basis, which means that the farmers are paid only after the vegetables are sold, while traders will pay at the time of purchase. In addition, retailers apply a deduction for "wastage" to account for produce that is spoiled in transit or cannot be sold. Finally, retailers may charge either a "rent" for vegetables sold in bins, or a "slotting fee" for vegetables on the supermarket shelves. Nevertheless, the prices earned by selling directly to retailers do appear to exceed those achieved from selling to intermediaries because of the savings in intermediary costs.

Although some institutional buyers and retailers (e.g., hypermarket chains) are shifting toward buying directly from farmers, the intermediaries are still the primary channels of farmers for marketing their vegetables. Intermediary costs comprise a significant percentage in the overall price; hence, farmers can increase their share of the final selling price by developing direct sales to consumers (footnote 3). SDC's VEGI Report (2016) discusses the need for establishing an effective vegetable wholesale market to improve competition (footnote 13).

One of the main reasons that farmers are not readily able to skip intermediaries is that they are unable to keep their perishable produce for an extended period of time without access to storage facilities. Therefore, they opt to sell these products as quickly and as efficiently as possible during the peak production period—which is the least profitable period for farmers (footnote 13). This eventually leads to weakness in vegetable prices. According to the World Bank, the most constraining marketing factors for Mongolian crop producers are low prices, followed by the presence of numerous market competitors (footnote 3). When smallholder farmers with backyard operations bring their vegetables to the market at the same time of the year, this leads to intense competition and dramatic price drops.

The lack of storage also limits farmers' potential to grow different types of vegetable varieties for longer periods (footnote 13). A possible solution could be for smallholder farmers to share storage facilities, which are too expensive for a single smallholder farmer. In this way, they could store their vegetables and provide supplies over an extended period, instead of selling all their produce to intermediaries as soon as they harvest them in autumn. However, it should be noted that locating storage on farms has disadvantages in that it does not increase the number of purchasers potentially buying the farmers' vegetables. The farmers still essentially rely on the same number of traders to purchase their produce. They can, however, store their produce for a while depending on the type of vegetable (leafy greens have to be sold quickly to attract premium prices), and the nature of the storage facility used (cold storage increases shelf life, but costs considerably more to construct).

The unit costs may also be higher for smaller storage facilities than for those that can accommodate a larger number of growers in a centralized location closer to the market. The formation of farmers' groups has had mixed consequences; although, in general, these groups are observed to achieve higher economies of scale than farmers acting individually.[14] Group formation also allows farmers more access to agricultural inputs and extension services, enhanced produce quality, and more effective business negotiations. Access of smallholder farmers to some shared storage facilities is justified, but the economics of this should be evaluated if access to alternative large-scale wholesale center facilities becomes available.

With intermediaries typically being their first and last marketing source, smallholder farmers do not develop the marketing skills and knowledge to add value to and market their products. Opening up additional sales channels may provide new opportunities to reach retailers, other large buyers, and possibly end users directly. Large supermarket representatives consulted during this study stressed that local smallholder farmers need to learn and adopt strong marketing practices, such as product branding, to draw support from large supermarkets.

Making food safety regulations and standards easier for farmers to use in their marketing activities could also assist in generating higher sales values. While there are laws, regulations, and standards, smallholder farmers are not able to use these effectively to enhance their products' attributes (footnote 13). Consumer demands for food quality and assurance are growing (footnote 14). Giving farmers clear guidelines, risk management training, or other necessary training and technical support would allow them to provide good quality and safe products that meet regulation requirements and standards as well as increase their competitive advantage. When farmers start labeling and packaging their products, they may be able to sell vegetables directly to retailers, institutional buyers, processors, and consumers; and they can save on costs, or sell at higher prices than via intermediaries.

Finally, it must be noted that the above analysis relates to price margins or "spreads" between key participants along the value chain. However, these are not profit margins per se, as they do not consider the costs for each participant in handling, transforming, or selling vegetables along the value chain. Farm data gathered for the purposes of modelling value chains suggest that profits, measured as vegetable revenues minus cash farm costs, vary according to the size and location of the farm. In general, the ratio of vegetable cash profit to sales is marginal for household growers with small farm size of under 1 ha, but ratio goes up to 60% for medium-scale farmers and/or growers with farm size of up to 20 ha. For processing, as per consulting team's estimates, pre-tax income as a percentage of sales is roughly 20%, which is normal for many agricultural raw material processing sectors. For retailing, vegetables also generate a margin over raw material costs of around 20%. However, once costs associated with sorting, packing, handling, and payment of value-added tax (which are not paid by farmers and, hence, are not claimable by retailers) are added, profits are marginal. Retailers in Mongolia can use vegetables as a loss leader to encourage customer traffic.

---

[14]   A. Shepherd. 2007. *Approaches to Linking Producers to Markets*. Vol. 13. Rome: Food and Agriculture Organization of the United Nations.

3.3.2   Procurement Sources, Producers, and Sources of Raw Materials

Table 36 estimates the percentage of total demand, by volume, procured for retail sales in each value chain based on the knowledge and information gathered by the consulting team during the course of the project.

Table 36: Share of Main Value Chains in Total Demand for Retail Sales in Mongolia

Main Value Chain		Percentage of Total Estimated Demand (%)
Value Chain 1	Smallholder farmers and/or individual growers—traders and/or large suppliers—wholesalers—markets and/or supermarkets (retailers)—consumers	50
Value Chain 2	Large and/or medium-scale farmers—name stores, supermarkets, or other retail points—consumers	10
Value Chain 3	Importers—traders and/or large suppliers—wholesalers—markets and/or supermarkets (retailers)—consumers	25
Value Chain 4	Smallholder farmers and/or individual growers or importers—processing factories—markets and/or supermarkets (retailers)—consumers	10
Value Chain 5	Smallholder farmers and/or individual growers or large and/or medium-scale farmers—large retailer "C"—consumers (direct procurement model)	5

Note: Large retailer "C" refers to a fairly new supermarket entrant who procures vegetables directly from farmers, subject to specified standards and norms.

Source: Consulting team analysis.

3.3.3   Evaluation of Imported Crops and Raw Materials, Prospects of Competition, and Scope for Import Substitution

Overall vegetable consumption in Mongolia is very restricted due to climate constraints and a lack of advanced farming techniques. In practice, the growth season for cultivated plants is considered to be about 90 days in central agricultural zones and about 110 days in the southern part of Mongolia where soil capacity and humidity factors for plant growth are less favorable for agriculture. This estimation of growth days was calculated based on the frost sensitivity of wheat in its early developmental stages. However, this information is now directly applied to the cultivation plans of most vegetable growers; therefore, most farmers believe vegetable cultivation should start in the middle of May. Table 21 provided precise estimates of planting and seeding days and growth lengths based on LDT and longitudinal climate data for some vegetables in project implementing *soums*. Along with the short growing season, there are climate factors that restrict plant growth in Mongolia. The most significant of these are drought, frost, wind, and soil fertility. Smallholder growers, who play the most active role in vegetable farming businesses, have limited economic access to enhance their productivity to offset climate constraints. Thus, imported vegetables play a significant role in total vegetable consumption.

According to the Customs General Administration of Mongolia, in 2017, more than 16 types of vegetables, including potatoes, were registered as imported (Table 37). The total volume of imported potatoes was 1.1 kt, and the total volume of imported vegetables was 75.2 kt. Cabbage, carrot, and onion were the imported vegetables with the highest volumes. These vegetables are considered the most commonly consumed and domestically cultivated vegetables in Mongolia. However, due to a lack of advanced cultivation techniques, limited storage facilities, and poorly developed transportation and value chain linkages for crop farming, the production of these vegetables is limited. Imported vegetables are currently filling the gap between domestic market supply and demand.

Although market demand is high, some of the most perishable vegetables that need to be consumed fresh, such as cucumber, mushroom, and tomato, are the least imported vegetables. Contributing factors include a lack of convenient storage facilities along transportation routes.

Importing companies spent $15.8 million on importing potatoes and vegetables during 2017, indicating a market gap that could be filled by domestically produced products. Some preliminary results of climate data and alternative crops analysis indicate a potential to significantly increase production by introducing climate-resilient technologies such as greenhouses, irrigation systems, and mechanization. Introduction of crops that are not currently grown in Mongolia, or grown only in small quantities, could also substitute for imports, although this will likely require a longer lead time. The potential for substitution of imports through expansion of production in current or alternative crops is covered in this report's technical analysis.

Table 37: Summary of Vegetables Imported into Mongolia, 2017

	Item	Amount (ton)	% in Amount of Vegetables	Value ($'000)	% in Value of Vegetables
1	Potato	1,144.65		219.43	
2	**Cabbage**	**17,541.76**	23.32	**3,108.45**	19.94
3	Mushroom	37.17	0.05	100.32	0.64
4	Onion	17,071.90	22.69	3,620.02	23.22
5	Lettuce, salad	6,410.46	8.52	1,356.28	8.70
6	Garlic	326.20	0.43	196.83	1.26
7	Carrot	10,146.60	13.49	1,829.24	11.73
8	<u>Turnip</u>	<u>32.29</u>	0.04	<u>5.13</u>	0.03
9	Tomato	718.59	0.96	192.30	1.23
10	Pepper	5,249.80	6.98	1,586.74	10.18
11	Cucumber	728.66	0.97	169.21	1.09
12	Other	339.40	0.45	189.43	1.21
13	Bok choy	6,121.06	8.14	1,110.89	7.13
14	Spinach	2,847.49	3.78	591.39	3.79
15	Melon	6,640.57	8.83	1,328.07	8.52
16	Eggplant	1,022.01	1.36	207.01	1.33
	Total	**76,378.62**		**15,810.74**	

Notes:

1. In this table, the highest volume and value of vegetables are in bold, and the lowest volume and value are underlined.
2. Numbers may not sum precisely, and percentages may not total 100%, because of rounding.

Source: Team analysis using field survey data.

3.3.4   Sources of Critical Inputs and Technologies

Vegetable consumption by the Mongolian population is increasing due to urbanization and increased knowledge among the general population of the requirements of a healthy diet, as demonstrated in the research undertaken by the NSO and the Ministry of Health in 2016. According to a food intake study, people in urban areas were consuming 30.3 g more of vegetables daily than those in rural areas (Table 38). In addition, vegetable consumption as a component of food intake increased from 171.3 kt in 2013 to 184.2 kt in 2016 (Table 39).

Table 38: Daily Potato and Vegetable Intake for Standard Population in Urban and Rural Areas
(gram)

Type	Urban Population	Rural Population
Potato	85.9	84.1
Vegetables	82.1	51.8

Source: National Statistical Office of Mongolia.

Table 39: Annual Food Demand for Standard Population, 2013–2016
(kiloton per year)

Food Category	Annual Food Consumption			
	2013	2014	2015	2016
Meat and meat products	171.3	174.7	180.8	184.2
Milk	128.6	131.1	135.7	138.3
Dairy products	171.3	174.7	180.8	184.2
Flour	85.7	87.3	90.4	92.1
All types of rice	188.5	192.1	198.9	202.6
Flour products	66.9	68.2	70.6	71.9
Sugar, sweetener	19.7	20.1	20.8	21.2
Potato	119.9	122.3	126.6	129.0
Vegetables	171.3	174.7	180.8	184.2
Fruits and berries	154.2	157.2	162.7	165.8
Pulses	77.2	78.7	81.5	83.0
Egg	16.2	16.5	17.1	17.4
Edible oil	21.4	21.8	22.5	23.0

Source: Ministry of Health.

To meet the increased demand for vegetables, it is necessary to introduce new types and varieties of vegetables, as well as advanced agribusiness technologies, with the support of value chain development. Vegetable production is considered to be a business by Mongolia's smallholder growers. Various techniques and equipment are necessary to support the development of advanced vegetable farming techniques and value-added products. These include

- irrigation systems (wells, channels, head works, drip irrigation, and cost-effective sprinkle irrigation for field growth; and drip and mist irrigation for greenhouses);

- agricultural machinery (soil cultivators, cultipackers, chisel plows, harrows, plows, rotators, rollers, seed drills, manure and chemical sprayers, conveyors, farm trucks, mowers, and tractors);

- cover growth techniques (many types of greenhouses and plastic domes: summer, 3-season, winter greenhouses, and glasshouses);

- climate-controlled storage facilities; and

- vegetable processing equipment.

The list of imported vegetables in Table 40 indicates high demand for many varieties of vegetables and value-added products, including dried and frozen vegetables and spices. Table 40 shows that vegetable import companies spent more than $95,000 in 2017 to import 67.5 tons of value-added products. One area of opportunity to support improved vegetable production is investment in processing industries for dried and frozen end products. For dried chopped vegetables, any type of food dehydrators, with costs ranging from $100 to $250 for households (e.g., Nesco brand) or from $7,000 to $18,000 for medium-scale farmers (e.g., TSM or Harvest Saver), can be used. For frozen chopped vegetables, instant freezers of below −18°C are recommended. Prices for instant freezers range from $1,500 to $3,000 for small-scale farmers, and from $10,000 to $50,000 for medium-scale farmers.

Table 40: Value-Added Imported Vegetable Products, 2017

Item	Amount (kilogram)	Value ($)
Peas, dried	6,325.25	3,654.56
Peas, frozen	5,350.00	4,398.43
Mixed frozen vegetables	38,761.70	35,584.28
Dried vegetables	1,711.99	23,803.71
Beans, frozen	5,040.00	3,994.28
Beans, mixed	27.24	89.93
Corn, frozen	3,246.00	2,753.47
Corn, dried	8.80	30.37
Coriander, dried	2,517.50	4,773.80
Dill, dried	1,067.70	7,553.99
Oregano, dried	151.20	2,073.84
Spices	1,666.12	4,349.04
Basil, dried	173.60	1,591.04
Ginger, dried	1,500.00	656.64
Total	**67,547.10**	**95,307.37**

Source: Customs General Administration of Mongolia.

3.4   Role of Smallholder Farmers in Meeting Value Chain Needs

Many consumers, restaurants, and schools are willing to purchase vegetables directly from Mongolian farmers rather than from Chinese imports due to their higher quality and freshness. However, the supply of domestically grown, highly nutritional, and value-added vegetables is only available from July to September. Therefore, purchasers obtain vegetables mainly from major wholesale market traders such as Bars Wholesale markets. Another issue is that potential new buyers must rely on year-round availability of vegetables, regardless of quality and origin. Cheap vegetables imported from the People's Republic of China outcompete domestic growers' vegetables by being accessible all year-round in close proximity to consumers. Therefore, Mongolian farmers, especially household vegetable growers, do not have any incentive to improve their farming technology, such as through investing in greenhouses.

Potential new buyers and market options include selling directly to restaurant chains, supermarkets, school caterers, dormitories, local farmers' markets, roadside farm stalls, and retail shops. Most of these are analyzed in section 4.2 in the value chain models. However, a separate investigation was undertaken into the potential for smallholder farmers to supply schools, dormitories, and similar institutions. Some vegetable growers in Bornuur noted that there were limited opportunities to supply to schools and similar institutional markets, and such opportunities, when they arose, were not tendered and awarded in a transparent way. Global Communities, an international nongovernment organization (NGO), has been successful in securing opportunities for its cooperatives to supply to local schools. However, it attributes this success to the fact that its cooperatives provide both dairy and vegetable products. The NGO further observed that, due to the seasonality of vegetable growing, vegetables could only be provided at limited times throughout the year.

4 TECHNICAL ANALYSIS: CONNECTING SMALLHOLDER FARMERS TO MARKETS

4.1 Introduction

To inform this section of the report, the consulting team produced a model that identifies the main revenue and cost components of vegetable growers for small-sized (< 3 ha) and medium-sized (3–30 ha) farms in each of the four target *soums* and Ulaanbaatar City. Information for this base case model was derived from farm surveys in the *soums* and Ulaanbaatar and field visits to the *soums* during late May 2018 to early June 2018.

This model has been used to assess the impacts of alternative cropping options on growers at the farm level (the alternative crops model).

The value chain analysis identified potential savings in costs and increases in revenue to farmers under a series of models for improved value chains (value chain model). These value chains are intended to reduce transaction costs and increase farm unit sales revenue through supply of vegetables from (i) farms to farm stalls, (ii) farms to processing, (iii) farms to retailing, and (iv) farms to central wholesaling and warehousing.

The impact analysis has been extended to determine what actions and investments are required by key private and public sector participants to realize the potential benefits of the improved value chains.

4.2 Models for Potential Improvement of Smallholder Community Grower Groups in Project *Soums* to Meet Market Needs

The modelling for this project has essentially been undertaken in three parts:

(i) Production of the current or base case;
(ii) Application of several technical changes (such as use of greenhouses, irrigation, and mechanization) to improve output and allow alternative cropping options for farmers (the alternative crops model); and
(iii) Application of several changes in the value chains, which increase prices received by farmers (the value chain models).

While the models for technical and value chain changes have been produced separately, they should be considered as being largely interdependent. It is unlikely that farmers will be able to effect value chain changes without technical changes in production. For example, to meet the demand of retailers for reliable year-round production, farmers would need to have access to summer and (especially) winter greenhouses, as well as irrigation and mechanization.

Similarly, technical changes will largely require value chain changes. Without the latter, farmers will continue to experience the impact of the bargaining power of intermediaries and retailers in terms of higher costs and lower revenues. Unless farmers can increase prices and offset the impact of increased output through value chain changes, any significant increase in output could lead to lower prices, especially in local markets.

In each case, results are summarized in physical and financial terms, with returns calculated for the farmers (and subsequent discussion of implications for other value chain participants).

4.2.1   Base Case Model

For the base case model, the key parameters and assumptions are as follows:

- Areas grown vary from 0.8 ha for a household farm in Ulaangom to 20 ha for a medium-sized farm in Bornuur and Yeruu.

- Production systems are a mix of open field, summer greenhouses, and winter greenhouses.

- Output volumes vary from 10,000 kg/year to 250,000 kg/year.

- All farms consume some of their own vegetables—up to 25% of production.

- Prices achieved, on average, from the sale of vegetables to traders vary from MNT600/kg to MNT1,000/kg.

- Generally, higher prices are achieved by household farms in the four *soums*, but for small volumes.

- Prices from traders are generally higher than those from wholesalers and retailers, but these are for small opportunistic volumes, and larger volume sales are at lower prices.

- The majority of sales in most areas go through wholesalers; but, in Orkhon, they go through handlers, and for household farms in Ulaangom, they go through traders.

- Significantly higher prices are achieved for sales by Ulaanbaatar farms due to winter greenhouse production.

- Vegetable revenue in some areas is supplemented by non-vegetable income such as consulting, other goods and services, and rental income.

- In Ulaanbaatar, the addition of non-vegetable income results in small vegetable cash income surpluses of around MNT0.522 million for household farms, and around MNT24.5 million for medium-sized farms.

- Excluding Ulaanbaatar, the average price weighted by volume through sales channels varies from MNT465/kg to MNT840/kg across the *soums*, and unit costs vary from MNT208/kg to MNT651/kg.

- Vegetable sales vary from MNT6 million (household farm in Ulaangom) to MNT120 million (medium-sized farm in Bornuur).

- Vegetable revenue varies from MNT6 million to MNT119 million, and costs from MNT4.6 million to MNT51 million.

- Cash income surplus from vegetable farming activities varies from breakeven results of around MNT13 million in all household farms to MNT67 million for medium-sized farms in Yeruu.

- Relative to sales, the vegetable cash income surplus is generally around 35%–60% for medium-sized farms.

4.2.2 Alternative Crops Model

The key assumptions of the alternative crops model are investment in summer and winter greenhouses; construction of wells, irrigation canals, and various types of irrigation systems (sprinkle, drip, and mist); tractor with aggregates; manure sprayers; and climate-controlled storage houses. The number of proposed investments varies based on farm sizes (Table 41). For example, the project consulting team proposes that three smallholder farmers share one large-sized winter greenhouse; whereas, a medium-sized farm owns a smaller winter greenhouse. For storage houses, two medium-sized farmers or 10 smallholder farmers will share a storage house with capacity of 100 tons. Regardless of farm sizes, two farmers will share tractors and manure sprayers. The technical change will bring a 620% increase in total output among the farmers of the four project *soums* compared to the base case model, and a 300% increase in total operational cost.

Table 41: Number of Proposed Investments Based on Farm Size

Investment Type	Medium-Sized Farm	Small-Sized Farm
Summer greenhouse, 120 m²	4	1
Winter greenhouse, 200 m²	1	–
Winter greenhouse, 600 m²	–	0.3
Well construction	1	1
Irrigation canal	1	1
Sprinkle irrigation	1	1
Drip irrigation	1	1
Mist irrigation	1	3
Tractor with aggregates	0.5	0.5
Manure sprayer	0.5	0.5
Storage house	0.5	0.1

– = not required, m² = square meter.
Note: Small-sized farm has <3 hectares of landholding, while medium-sized farm has 3–30 hectares.
Source: Team analysis using field survey data.

For the alternative crops model, the key parameters and assumptions are outlined below:

■ Total vegetable revenue varies from MNT44.1 million to MNT867.1 million across the *soums*.

■ Vegetable cash income surplus varies from MNT25.5 million to MNT659.5 million across the *soums*, with all *soums* recording a positive cash income surplus.

■ Relative to sales, the vegetable farm income surplus varies from 47% to 78% across the *soums*.

■ Investment costs are MNT301 million for medium-sized farms and MNT180 million for small-sized farms in each *soum*.

■ Payback periods vary from 0.5 years to 7.5 years, and net present values (NPVs) (without loans) are positive within 3–5 years only for medium-sized farms.

■ Based on 45 farms per *soum* in community grower groups (CGGs) for the project, the total investment costs are MNT43,236 million ($18.0 million). This is equivalent to $100,000 per farm for 180 farms (i.e., 30 CGGs, each with six farms).

Based on the substantial increases in vegetable production under this model, the combined outputs from the four project *soums* should increase from the 2016 estimate of 27,000 tons to volumes almost on a par with the current national production of vegetables and, therefore, would easily replace the 2016 level of imports.

4.2.3 Value Chain Models

The value chains modelled in the technical analysis of this report include the following:

■ **Farm stall.** The farm stall model was considered for all four project *soums*. Altogether, 30 stalls will be established (seven or eight for each *soum*), located either along busy local roads and transport hubs (e.g., train and bus stations, service points) or at the Ulaanbaatar City market, the main vegetable market in the country. It was assumed that the vegetable unit sales prices would be highest in the farm stall and the wholesale center models compared to the other two value chain models.

■ **Processor.** Direct supply to the processor is being considered for Orkhon. It is assumed that an established and experienced private sector company with substantial market share shall establish one new vegetable processing facility at Orkhon. Moreover, it is assumed that farmers from other project *soums* shall supply processors (mainly located in Ulaanbaatar) directly without intermediaries. The farmers shall be responsible for the transportation and, as such, delivery costs are added.

■ **Retailer.** Direct supply to retailers was considered for both small and medium-sized producers from all project *soums*. It is assumed that the major retailers shall be based mainly in Ulaanbaatar. Similar to the processor value chain model, the farmers shall take care of the transportation; consequently, delivery costs are added.

- **Wholesale center.** The wholesale center model is more relevant for farmers in Bornuur, Orkhon, and Yeruu. However, it is assumed that a similar model would also be functional in Ulaangom. A novel, modern, and food safety-assured wholesale center with full logistics, storage, and access solutions shall be built at a strategically advantageous location, and will serve as a vegetable supply hub for Ulaanbaatar. This is the role that is currently served by Bars markets, which have been subject to several concerns, including health and safety issues. The assumption is that the wholesale center will become the place to connect all sizes and types of farmers with individual, retail, public sector, and institutional consumers, enabling a "win-win" scenario for all parties. Data will be centrally collected on sales transactions and communicated to facilitate transparency. Transactions, logistical, and other data can be handled through an advanced blockchain system.

Similar assumptions were applied to all four value chains , and these are as follows:

- On-farm consumption will be reduced to nil to maximize profits.

- Due to the remoteness of Ulaangom from Ulaanbaatar and the prohibitively high transportation costs, it is assumed that the relevant value chain models are still applicable, but within a local market context.

- The model for CGGs could be the Greenhouse Vegetable Growers Federation, which currently provides capacity building, knowledge transfer, and other professional and advisory services, but could also encompass ownership of assets (including brands) with appropriate support.

- All prices quoted in the base case are the consulting team's best conservative estimate based on market study and value chain price spreads. There is no price or volume differentiation between individual vegetables in the base case model at each farm, which makes it difficult to accurately estimate the potential price in the value chain models. However, the consulting team used common sense and local market knowledge in this exercise to construct estimates.

- CGG costs (recouped in full from farmers) are MNT1.6 million, based on current estimated costs for servicing a farmer member of the Greenhouse Vegetable Growers Federation.

- Transportation costs are assumed to be MNT76/kg, as per consultant team's estimations (valid within 300 kilometers of the destination market).

- The price in MNT/kg sold to the end-consumer is the consulting team's best conservative estimate, based on market and value chain analyses. The increase in unit price as a result of reduction in intermediary costs in each value chain model was calculated by comparing the "price in MNT/kg sold weighted by sales channel" figures in the respective value chain versus the base case. The increase in sales revenue, however, takes into account the volumes sold through each sales channel and, thus, represents better value for comparison.

Table 42 presents the key assumptions of the four value chain models.

Table 42: Key Assumptions of the Value Chain Models

Value Chain Model	Key Assumptions
Farm stall	All rural farms will sell 50% of their produce directly to end-consumers through stall sales.
	Ulaanbaatar-based medium-sized farms will sell 60%, while small-sized farms will sell 90%, of their produce through farm stalls, taking advantage of the benefit of market proximity.
	No breakdown of volume of products sold through local or Ulaanbaatar stalls was considered.
Processor	Farmers will sell 30%–100% of their harvest to processors based on the location and size of the farm.
	The above assumption is interlinked with potential sales prices to ensure maximum profit scenario for the farm(er).
	Except for Orkhon *soum*, a seasonal vegetable procurement center will be established, and a full-time procurement agent will purchase vegetables every 4 months per year.
Retailer	Farmers shall supply at least 50%, and up to 90%, of their produce directly to retailers, skipping intermediaries.
	The variation in the percentage of harvest sold to retailers depends on the location and potential prices farmers could fetch by supplying to a specific sales channel, always maximizing farmers' profits.
	All farmers in the project *soums* would need packaging and packing equipment to enable them to directly supply to retailers. Another potential expense, the branding and labeling slotting fee, is assumed to be 20% of retail price (as appears to be the normal practice in Mongolia), and is considered an investment cost.
	The price per unit of sales of branded product would need to increase by 20%, other things being equal, to compensate for the slotting fees. The price per unit and slotting fees would be a matter for negotiation between the farmer and/or community grower group and the retailer concerned, with the outcome determined by their respective bargaining powers.
Wholesale center	Farmers shall sell from 50% to 100% of their produce through the wholesale center.
	Farmers shall be able to fetch higher prices for vegetables, compared to the processor and retailer models, due to direct sale, comfort, and convenience to the customer who shops at the new wholesale center.
	Sales prices will be 15% lower compared to the stalls model.
	There is no rental cost assumed for farmers to sell at the wholesale center; any such costs would depend on the cost recovery policies of the government and would serve to reduce farm cash vegetable income accordingly.

Notes:
1. Small-sized farm has <3 hectares of landholding, while medium-sized farm has 3–30 hectares.
2. *Soum* is a subprovincial administrative unit in Mongolia, which is equivalent to a district.

Source: Team analysis using field survey data.

The key parameters of the models are outlined in Table 43 and summarized as follows:

- All of the value chains increase vegetable income relative to the base case; the biggest percentage increase being in medium-sized farms in Yeruu, which were breakeven in the base case.

- The increases in vegetable income in percentage terms are generally larger for the farm stall and the wholesale center models because the percentage increase in revenue from removing intermediaries is larger in these cases. This is because direct sales would enable farmers to fetch higher unit prices compared to the other two models, and it also reflects the volumes of products supplied to that specific sales channel. With the processor and the retailer value chain models, a price ceiling is already indicated as per the base model, while with the farm stall and the wholesale center models, the consulting team has been able to estimate the increase.

- Relative to sales, the vegetable farm income surplus is positive in all the value chains and the values are similar to those for the alternative crops model.

- Increases in the vegetable income relative to sales for all the value chains are somewhat higher for the farm stall and the wholesale center models than the processor and the retailer models (but overall, they are quite similar to the increase under the alternative crops model).

- The total investment costs (private sector) amount to MNT60 million for the farm stall model, MNT9.8 billion for the processor model, and MNT151.9 million for the retailer model, while investment costs (public sector) for the wholesale center model are MNT147 billion.

4.2.3.1 Key Conclusions

The alternative crops model results in substantial increases in output compared with the base case. The increases in revenue significantly exceed the increases in operational costs, raising farmers' vegetable cash incomes. These revenue increases are based on the technical changes producing the calculated results immediately and with no impact on prices. The measures to be introduced are technically feasible and currently in use in Mongolia. The application of some technologies assumes that CGGs own or manage the assets. Such groups could be based on existing organizations, and some current initiatives supported by other development partners will yield insights. Finally, this model requires considerable asset investments. However, the returns on these investments are modest, payback periods vary from 0.5 years to 7.5 years, and NPVs (without loans) would be positive within 3–5 years for medium-sized farms alone. In effect, the costs of increasing production to enable value chain changes that produce price gains for farmers are loaded onto the alternative crops model.

The value chain models produce improved prices and incomes for farms by reducing intermediaries. This assumes that volume and other supply requirements of the purchasers have been met. Critically, it also assumes that farmers capture all the gains that result from eliminating intermediaries. Ultimately, the prices that farmers will receive from direct sales to consumers at stalls, direct sales to processors and retailers, and sales at a wholesale center will be determined by the commercial negotiations that take place between the parties concerned. This requires consideration of the relative

Table 43: Key Parameters of the Value Chain Models

Value Chain Model	Bornuur		Yeruu		Ulaangom		Orkhon		Total
	Medium-Sized Farm	Household Farm	Medium-Sized Farm	Household Farm	Medium-Sized Farm	Household Farm	Medium-Sized Farm	Household Farm	Average
Farm-Stall Model									
% increase in price from reduced intermediaries	129%	131%	136%	128%	160%	134%	131%	138%	136%
% increase in sales revenue	140%	143%	146%	130%	176%	141%	163%	140%	147%
% increase in sales from reduced on-farm consumption	109%	109%	107%	102%	110%	105%	124%	102%	108%
% increase in costs									
Due to rental of stalls	0.3%	1.0%	0.5%	1.3%	0.5%	1.8%	0.3%	0.8%	0.8%
Due to extra transportation to operate stalls	11.6%	3.6%	6.3%	5.9%	7.9%	5.6%	8.6%	8.0%	7.0%
Investment costs, MNT'000									
Cost of stalls		15,000		15,000		15,000		15,000	60,000
Farm-Processor Model									
% increase in price from reduced intermediaries	115%	119%	125%	115%	112%	119%	116%	129%	119%
% increase in sales revenue	125%	130%	133%	117%	123%	125%	144%	131%	129%
% increase in costs									
Due to transportation to processors	17.4%	7.1%	9.2%	9.2%	9.4%	3.5%	11.4%	13.4%	10%
Investment costs, MNT'000									
Processing plant								9,800,000	9,800,000
Vegetable procurement center, staff hired for 4 months with monthly salary of MNT700,000		2,800		2,800		2,800			8,400
Farm-Retailer Model									
% increase in price from reduced intermediaries	115%	107%	119%	113%	106%	109%	116%	123%	114%
% increase in sales revenue	125%	117%	127%	115%	116%	115%	144%	125%	123%
% increase in costs									
Due to transportation to retailers	17.0%	3.0%	7.0%	8.0%	6.0%	5.0%	12.0%	11.0%	9%
Investment costs, MNT'000									
Packing equipment		37,975		37,975		37,975		37,975	151,900
Branding and labeling	20% slotting fee								
Vehicles		10,000		10,000		10,000		10,000	40,000

continued on next page

Table 43 *continued*

Value Chain Model	Bornuur		Yeruu		Ulaangom		Orkhon		Total
	Medium-Sized Farm	Household Farm	Medium-Sized Farm	Household Farm	Medium-Sized Farm	Household Farm	Medium-Sized Farm	Household Farm	
Farm–Wholesale Center Model									
% increase in price from reduced intermediaries	146%	131%	158%	144%	192%	141%	144%	172%	154%
% increase in sales revenue	159%	143%	169%	147%	211%	148%	179%	175%	166%
% increase in costs									
Transport	3.0%	3.0%	2.0%	2.0%	5.0%	4.0%	9.0%	15.0%	5%
Investment costs, MNT'000									
Feasibility study valued at current market price of $100,000									245,000
Wholesale center, adopted from Melbourne sample at $60 million to 70 ha center									147,000,000
For All Models									
CGG costs, MNT'000	200	200	200	200	200	200	200	200	1,600
Increase in farm costs from CGG activities (services only) per farm for six farms									
Capacity building									
Knowledge transfer									
Other services									
Elimination of intermediaries costs									
Farmers capture all of price margin due to intermediaries elimination									100%

CGG = community grower group, ha = hectare, MNT = Mongolian togrog.
Note: Household farm has <3 ha of landholding, while medium-sized farm has 3–30 ha.
Source: Team analysis using field survey data.

bargaining power of farmers and purchasers along the supply chain. Indeed, increased production, as envisaged under the alternative crops model, could also increase downward pressure on prices if bargaining power is unbalanced. There is a need to evaluate the current competition laws as they relate to smallholder farmers' dealings with purchasers, including the potential for introducing fair trading legislation and standard form contracts to ensure farmers can benefit from value chain changes. Finally, the asset investments required to generate benefits for farmers largely occur further along the value chain. However, the point about loading technology costs onto the alternative crops model should again be noted.

4.2.4 Key Constraints for Market Entry and Access to High-Value Markets

Farmers are constrained from accessing or entering high-value markets by their inability to supply adequate volumes over the period required. The application of technologies in the alternative crops model is aimed at addressing this constraint. However, the costs of applying the technologies are substantial and the returns will need to be augmented by improvements in value chains. The value chain models aim to address these constraints. In addition, smallholder farmers are unlikely to have the capital required to make such investments in the first place. A loan program that provides access to capital on concessionary terms will help improve returns.

A further set of constraints relate to product quality. The vegetable supply is time-critical and farmers need to be able to ensure that their transport facilities allow vegetables to reach buyers in prime condition.

Farmers also need to ensure their produce meets the food safety requirements of all relevant laws and the specific additional demands of buyers. Unfortunately, farmers may view such specific requirements as onerous, and this reinforces the need for balanced competition conditions. Current regulatory requirements and practical application of soil testing need to ensure that farmers can meet commercial requirements at the lowest possible cost, including through improved recognition of the results of tests conducted for one buyer by other buyers. This requires both private and regulatory actions.

Another potential key constraint relates to the organizational structure, associated legal composition, and recognition of CGGs. Information gathered from the field by the project consulting team revealed that organizations registered as NGOs are not able to enter into contracts with supermarkets and other commercial organizations.

4.2.5 Actions to Overcome Constraints

Various investments, including high level identification of equipment and infrastructure requirements, are needed to overcome the constraints identified in section 4.2.4. The investments required at the farm level under the alternative crops model are presented in Table 44. Investments relating to the stages in the value chain at which they occur and the party responsible for investing are indicated in Table 45.

Table 44: Farm-Level Investments under the Alternative Crops Model
(MNT million)

Required Investment	Quantity Required (no.)	Unit Cost	Total Cost
Summer greenhouse	450	4.0	1,800.0
Winter greenhouse, small	90	75.8	6,822.0
Winter greenhouse, large	30	175.2	5,257.0
Storage	54	250.0	13,500.0
Others (e.g., mechanization, irrigation)	–	–	15,858.0
Total investment costs	–	–	43,237.0
$ million equivalent costs	–	–	18.0

– = not applicable, MNT = Mongolian togrog.
Note: Numbers may not sum precisely because of rounding.
Source: Team analysis using field survey data.

Table 45: Investments under the Value Chain Models
(MNT million)

Type of Investment	Quantity Required (no.)	Unit Cost	Farm Stall	Processor	Retailer	Wholesale	Investor
Farm stall	4	15.0	60.0				Government
Processing plant	1	9,800.0		9,800.0			Processor
Procurement center	3	2.8		8.4			Processor
Packaging equipment	4	38.0			152.0		Farm or CGG
Vehicle	4	10.0			40.0		Farm or CGG
Feasibility study for IOT	1	245.0				245.0	ADB
Wholesale center	1	147,000.0				147,000.0	Government

ADB = Asian Development Bank, CGG = community grower group, IOT = Internet of Things, MNT = Mongolian togrog.
Source: Team analysis using field survey data .

4.2.6 Farm-Level Economic Analysis and Financial Requirements

The farm-level impacts of the alternative crops model are indicated in Table 46. As pointed out in the key financial results, payback periods vary from 0.5 years to 7.5 years and NPVs (without loans) are positive within 3–5 years for medium-sized farms alone.

However, with a loan program based on the terms of the former Chinggis Bonds (7 years repayment at 8% interest), negative NPVs are reduced and positive NPVs are increased substantially.

Table 46: Farm-Level Impacts of the Alternative Crops Model
(MNT million)

Item	Bornuur		Yeruu		Ulaangom		Orkhon	
	Medium-Sized Farm	Household Farm	Medium-Sized Farm	Household Farm	Medium-Sized Farm	Household Farm	Medium-Sized Farm	Household Farm
Total investment cost per farm	301	180	301	180	301	180	301	180
Increased vegetable income of base case	592	34	114	35	188	24	354	56
Benefit/cost, year 1	2.0	0.2	0.4	0.2	0.6	0.1	1.2	0.3
Payback period (year)	0.5	5.2	2.6	5.1	1.6	7.5	0.8	3.2
Assuming all investment is loan-funded								
Loan for investment	301	180	301	180	301	180	301	180
Per annum, 7 years	43.0	25.6	43.0	25.6	39.9	25.6	39.9	25.6
Interest @ 8%	3.4	2.1	3.4	2.1	3.2	2.1	3.2	2.1
Yearly payment	46.4	27.7	46.4	27.7	43.1	27.7	43.1	27.7
No-Loan, Year 2								
IRR (%)	97%	(23%)	7%	(45%)	(37%)	(56%)	18%	(26%)
No. of years	2	4	4	3	2	3	2	3
NPV, MNT million @ 8%	698.6	(61.0)	72.4	(82.2)	162.6	(92.3)	306.7	(31.5)
No. of years	3	5	5	4	4	5	3	4
Loan, 7 years @ 8%								
IRR (%)	2195%		217%		521%		1209%	137%
NPV, MNT million @ 8%	2,247.0	(23.8)	203.7	(20.1)	520.5	(67.6)	1,231.2	71.0

( ) = negative value, IRR = internal rate of return, MNT = Mongolian togrog, NPV = net present value.
Note: Household farm has <3 hectares of landholding, while medium-sized farm has 3–30 hectares.
Source: Team analysis using field survey data.

Compared with the base case, vegetable farm income increases for all farmers would further improve returns, as indicated in Table 47. In this analysis, vegetable farm income is calculated as vegetable farming receipts minus costs.

Table 47: Income and Returns for All Models

Item	Bornuur		Yeruu		Ulaangom		Orkhon	
	Medium-Sized Farm	Household Farm	Medium-Sized Farm	Household Farm	Medium-Sized Farm	Household Farm	Medium-Sized Farm	Household Farm
Vegetable Income (MNT '000)								
Base Case	67,700	1,430	(852)	3,132	13,530	1,445	27,987	2,953
Alternative Crops	659,500	35,750	113,592	38,325	201,995	25,540	382,468	59,414
Farm-Stall	115,600	5,390	15,548	5,544	48,030	3,965	80,350	8,785
Farm-Processor	98,100	4,190	11,148	4,494	24,030	2,965	64,750	7,505
Farm-Retailer	98,100	2,990	8,748	4,344	21,030	2,365	64,750	6,545
Farm-Wholesale	138,100	5,390	23,948	6,894	64,030	4,365	93,550	13,905
Change in Vegetable Income from Base Case (%)								
Base Case	100	100	100	100	100	100	100	100
Alternative Crops	974	2,500	13,332	1,224	1,493	1,767	1,367	2,012
Farm-Stall	171	377	1,825	177	355	274	287	298
Farm-Processor	145	293	1,308	143	178	205	231	254
Farm-Retailer	145	209	1,027	139	155	164	231	222
Farm-Wholesale	204	377	2,811	220	473	302	334	471
Vegetable Income/Sales Returns (%)								
Base Case	57	13	(2)	39	30	24	34	20
Alternative Crops	69	40	27	57	50	46	53	43
Farm-Stall	69	41	30	54	60	46	59	43
Farm-Processor	65	35	23	48	43	39	54	39
Farm-Retailer	65	28	19	47	40	34	54	36
Farm-Wholesale	73	41	39	59	67	49	63	54
Change in Vegetable Income/Sales Returns from Base Case (%)								
Base Case	57	15	(2)	39	30	24	34	20
Alternative Crops	13	25	30	18	20	22	19	23
Farm-Stall	12	25	32	14	30	22	26	23
Farm-Processor	9	19	26	9	13	15	20	19
Farm-Retailer	9	12	22	8	10	10	20	16
Farm-Wholesale	16	25	42	19	37	25	29	34

( ) = negative value, MNT = Mongolian togrog.

Note: Household farm has < 3 hectares of landholding, while medium-sized farm has 3–30 hectares.

Source: Team analysis using field survey data.

4.3 Analysis of Input Supply, Processing, Marketing, and Distribution

The implications for the other relevant stages of the chain are as follows:

- For traders and other intermediaries, the development of direct sales from farmers to consumers (in the case of farm stalls), processors, retailers, and to a wholesale selling center, causes loss of income. The establishment of a new selling center potentially replaces the wholesale facilities currently in place.

- For processors, new investment in a plant is required in Orkhon.[15] This investment is assumed to replicate the new ADB-supported facility currently being developed in Ulaanbaatar. It can be assumed that the returns to that investment will be replicated in the additional facility.

- For retailers, the direct sales from farmers will reflect the current trend in place, which is driven by the retailers' needs for volume, year-round supply, and quality. One issue for resolution is whether the produce will carry the retailers' brand or the farmers' brand. Currently, most produce sold directly from farm to retailer carries the retailers' brand. An exception is the brand owned by a major integrated farming, wholesaling, or trading company. Produce supplied for retailers' own brands is generally sorted, cleaned, and packed by the retailer in-store or at a centralized logistics or packing facility. If the farmers or CGGs wish to supply their own brand, they will likely need to undertake sorting, cleaning, and packing. The assumptions for the retail value chain model include an estimate of the cost of an appropriate packaging investment. The retailer will also likely require payment of the standard 20% slotting fee to place the farmers' brand product on the shelf and promote it. Adequate returns will depend on (i) raising the price of the branded product sufficiently to exceed the 20% slotting fee, and (ii) achieving a return on the packaging asset investment at least equivalent to the cost of capital. Ultimately the price at which the farmer-branded product is sold will be determined by the relative bargaining power of the parties concerned. At least one retailer has indicated a willingness to negotiate around the branding issue and possibly develop a brand jointly with farmers. This opportunity should be explored and supported.

In a marketing sense, there is considerable potential for branded vegetable products, especially for higher-value produce like leafy greens. There appears to be strong underlying demand for domestically grown vegetables mainly due to concerns about the safety of some imported products. There is an opportunity for farmers to capitalize on this demand, but only if the food safety attributes of their produce can be backed up by appropriate evidence. This means that farmers and retailers should develop a shared understanding of what food safety measures are required, with complementary action by regulators.

---

[15]   This aligns with the activity included in the ADB-supported *Community Vegetable Farming for Livelihood Improvement Project* to establish a vegetable processing and packaging facility and/or workshop in the Orkhon *soum*. This is proposed to be equipped with relevant tools and small-scale machinery and equipment.

4.3.1 Key Constraints, Actions, and Investments by the Public and Private Sectors

The key constraints and actions required by the private and public sectors are summarized in Table 48.

Table 48: Key Constraints and Actions Required by the Private and Public Sectors

Key Constraint	Action	Private Sector	Public Sector
Lack of volume and year-round supply	Technical investment	Farmers	Investment financing
	Establish community grower groups		Training
Inadequate returns	Value chain changes	Value chain participants	Investment financing
	Fair trading conditions		Improve competition framework
Food safety	Agreed standards	Value chain participants	Regulation
Branding	Farmers brand development	Farmers and retailers	Improve competition framework

Source: Team analysis using field survey data.

4.3.2 Potential Establishment of Contract Arrangements to Facilitate Connecting the Community Grower Groups to Markets

In terms of vertical arrangements, there is considerable potential for the establishment of contract arrangements between farmers and processors, and between farmers and retailers, which will help reduce transaction costs and improve returns to farmers and retailers while meeting consumer needs. The establishment of a wholesale center would also facilitate direct sales between farmers and wholesalers, as well as to retailers.

To achieve this, farmers need to supply the volumes of produce required, at the time required, and in the required quality, including food safety. The government needs to implement a competition framework that facilitates a balance of bargaining power between the parties concerned.

In terms of horizontal arrangements, the establishment of CGGs would facilitate training and knowledge-sharing among farmers, promote economies of scale through joint ownership of assets and marketing of produce (including development of farmer-owned brands), and increase farmer bargaining power in vertical arrangements.

CGGs could be modelled on Greenhouse Vegetable Growers Federation and similar groups. They could form umbrella organizations to manage groups with varying numbers of farmers and cooperatives. The groups could own common assets such as greenhouses and storage facilities, where appropriate, and lease those assets to individual farmers. The groups would accordingly need to have legal status, enabling them to conduct such commercial activities and commensurate formal governance arrangements. They would require training and infrastructure support (such as appropriate office facilities) as well as support for legislative or regulatory changes.

The Sustainable Vegetable Production and Marketing (VEGI) Project pilot approach of the Swiss Agency for Development and Cooperation (SDC) is one example that the ADB-supported Community Vegetable Farming for Livelihood Improvement Project could monitor. This project targets the development of functioning contracts between cooperatives and the private sector. It has recently secured a contract with Nomin Supermarket, one of the first and largest supermarket chains in Ulaanbaatar and Mongolia, which serves approximately 1.2 million customers each day through 3 department stores, 10 wholesale stores, and 7 hypermarkets.

For this pilot, eight agricultural cooperatives from seven *soums* in four *aimags*, which were formed through the VEGI Project, have merged to form a secondary marketing cooperative under the common name of "Mongolian Vegetables." The secondary marketing cooperative aims to channel healthy vegetables directly from farm producers to end-consumers. It also seeks to promote contract farming, including capacity building of its members. A partnership memorandum of understanding was signed between the VEGI Project and Nomin Holdings in late December 2017 for a daughter company of Nomin Supermarket (the Nomin Tav Trade Supermarket) to purchase agricultural products from the VEGI secondary cooperative, without intermediary players, on the principles of contract farming.

Specifically, the secondary marketing cooperative comprises the eight primary marketing cooperatives and the two implementing agencies for the VEGI Project: the Mongolian Farmer Association for Rural Development (MFARD) and the Mongolian Women Farmers Association. This secondary marketing cooperative was officially incorporated in April 2018. According to the Law on Cooperatives, at least 51% of members should be cooperative members and the rest can be private companies and NGOs.

The secondary marketing cooperative is contracted to supply Nomin Supermarket with stored vegetables and potatoes twice per week. The main vegetables supplied will be carrots, beetroots, and potatoes, as well as fresh goods such as tomatoes when harvested. The volume of vegetables will depend on the season. Importantly, any supply shortfall by the primary marketing cooperatives could be met by private farmers or companies that are MFARD members.[16]

4.3.3   Key Constraints for Downstream Value Chain Participants

The major infrastructure, business, and investment actions required of downstream public and private participants can be summarized as follows:

- **Public sector.** Financing of investments under the alternative crops model, construction of farm stalls for the stalls value chain model, financing of a new facility in the processor value chain model, feasibility and construction of a wholesale selling center, training and infrastructure support for CGGs, and establishment of an enabling competition environment relating to vegetable supply would also be required.

- **Private sector.** Asset investments are required in all models, except for the wholesale selling center. Suggested key ownership and operating structure features for the wholesale selling center are as follows:

---

[16]   The MFARD is a member-oriented NGO with 1,300 individual farmer members nationwide; and its members are generally more open field growers than greenhouse vegetable farmers.

(i)   The facility should be developed and owned by the government but have a management board or committee with representation from farmers and other users of the facility.

(ii)   The design and operation of the center should reflect various models of wholesale centers in relevant countries, notably the Republic of Korea, which reportedly has a highly successful center.

(iii) The center should provide facilities for farmers and CGGs to sell produce as wholesalers in appropriately sized outlets, and for larger-scale wholesalers to sell produce to retailers. It should provide for both auctions and direct sales to facilitate as many options for value chain participants to access markets as possible and commercially practicable (dependent on volumes handled through the center).

(iv)   A critically important function of the center would be to gather, aggregate, and disseminate market information on volumes and prices. This information should form part of a larger "Internet of Things" platform that integrates logistics and trade, as well as facilitates traceback for food safety.

4.3.4 Feasibility of Improvements: Technical, Commercial, Financial, Social, and Scalability

All the improvements suggested in the various models are technically feasible, reflecting current technologies already in place in Mongolia. There is also the potential for carbon dioxide (CO_2) enhancement to increase production in greenhouses under the alternative crops model. CO_2 enhancement has the potential to increase yields by around 50%. Investments would be required for a facility to produce CO_2, transport to the farms, store, and circulate CO_2 in the greenhouses.

It is almost certain that concessional financing will be required for investment in the alternative crops model, given the significant amount of funds required, and the likely lack of access to capital on commercial terms by household and medium-sized vegetable farms. The investments required for the value chain models (except for the wholesale center) would be undertaken by private sector participants, but concessional financing for the additional processing facility would facilitate its establishment, as has been the case with the processing investment currently underway.

There are no significant issues associated with the social feasibility of the proposed improvements, and they are likely to generate significant benefits. Monitoring will be important to ensure that CGGs are developed and supported appropriately as organizational units that can effectively participate in project activities. Several key informants commented on the need to ensure that CGG members self-identify and voluntarily join together based on their own common and mutual interests rather than being formed by the Community Vegetable Farming for Livelihood Improvement Project, or the Ministry of Food, Agriculture and Light Industry (MOFALI). In other words, CGGs should respond to specific community interests and needs rather than being driven by the opportunity presented by the project. Further to this, other development projects tend to work with and support cooperatives rather than small CGGs, as cooperatives have a legal structure. This aspect may require further review by the Community Vegetable Farming for Livelihood Improvement Project as it begins to mobilize.

It would be valuable to monitor lessons learned and insights gained from the VEGI Project. For example, the VEGI Project conducted cooperatives strengthening training in 2017. This supported cooperative members to develop business plans and investment projects and undertake cost–benefit analyses. All trainees received handbooks and simplified accounting and finance software that cooperatives and individuals could use to manage and monitor their income and expenses. Specific leadership training was also provided for managers and monitoring boards of the marketing cooperatives.

It would also be of value for the Community Vegetable Farming for Livelihood Improvement Project to map, in consultation with MOFALI, (i) the various development partner, private sector, and NGO-supported initiatives planned or already underway in the four target *soums* for the project; and (ii) the broader social context of each. This process could identify potential leverage points for the new ADB-supported project as it mobilizes. For example, in Bornuur, the consulting team observed that (i) the VEGI Project is already present, with its own extension center that provides training and subsidized use of equipment and seeds to MFARD members; and (ii) the Japan International Cooperation Agency (JICA) has built a farmers' stall on the road to Bornuur through which locally produced vegetables and pickles will be sold. The Enabling Market Integration through Rural Group Empowerment (EMIRGE) Project, supported by the Government of the United States, is active in Darkhan-Uul, Selenge, and Tuv *aimags*, including in Bornuur and Orkhon *soums*. Among other activities, the EMIRGE Project provides practical training at the farm level on good agricultural and hygiene practices in consultation with the General Agency for Specialized Inspection. Artisanal mining activities are also prevalent in several target *soums*; for example, in Bornuur, artisanal miners often also undertake seasonable vegetable growing. This broader societal context may influence the effectiveness of ADB initiatives.

In addition to a *soum*-level focus, there may be other broader crossover points and potential opportunities for leverage. For example, in May 2018, several entities signed a memorandum to support the development of small and medium-sized enterprises (SMEs) in Mongolia by facilitating necessary training in various business practices. They include the International Finance Corporation (IFC), Oyu Tolgoi LLC, Deutsche Gesellschaft für Internationale Zusammenarbeit (GIZ), the Gobi Oyu Development Support Fund, and the Umnugovi governor.[17] The World Bank is preparing a National Livestock and Agriculture Commercialization Project using results-based financing. The European Bank for Reconstruction and Development is promoting agriculture and land farming and is supporting SMEs.

The improvements in all models are eminently scalable. Even the wholesale selling center could be scaled up, assuming that sufficient land and transport infrastructure are provided for in its design.

---

[17] *The UB Post*. 2018. Memorandum signed between IFC and development agencies to support SMEs. 18 May.

5

CONNECTING SMALLHOLDER VEGETABLE FARMERS TO MARKETS IN OTHER DEVELOPING CENTRAL ASIAN COUNTRIES

Through its sovereign and nonsovereign operations, ADB is supporting governments in other developing member countries in central Asia to connect smallholder vegetable farmers to markets. The general constraints and opportunities for the participation of farmers and farmer organizations are similar. Experiences and lessons learned from feasibility studies and ongoing or planned interventions have valuable implications for Mongolia.

5.1 Kazakhstan

An ADB-funded assessment of Kazakhstan's vegetable market systems estimates that around 5% of the total production is sold by smallholder farmers directly from their cars and small trucks outside of small retail markets (bazaar).[18] About 35% of the total production is sold to traders and then further distributed through wholesale markets. Around 30% of the production goes to processing industries, which collect directly at all sizes of farms, thereby bypassing wholesale markets. The farmers are financially weak and depend on cash immediately after having harvested their products. When offering their produce for sale, they are usually left with only one option—offering up-front cash payment. If farmers had stronger financial conditions or credit options, they would have the flexibility to postpone the sales or pursue alternative sales options. There is no flow of information backward in the value chain, so farmers are not aware of grades, quality, and prices, or which species to produce to maximize the value created. The insufficient farmer-to-market connection results in behavior leading to food wastage and low quality.

Attempts to establish local storage and cooling facilities have sometimes been successful. Failures have been due to the above-mentioned cash constraints, preventing farmers from postponing their sales. Attempts to establish collection centers as cooperatives have been carried out, but with very limited success. Cooperatives or sales associations are workable solutions to strengthening producers' positions in the value chain; however, in all cases, these initiatives require strong and competent farmers. An additional challenge with connecting smallholder farmers directly to wholesale markets is the presence of large operators that are active players in the buying and selling of produce.

---

[18]   ADB. 2017. *Knowledge and Support Technical Assistance (KSTA 51254-001): Almaty–Bishkek Economic Corridor Support.* Manila; and ADB. 2018. *Kazakhstan National Wholesale Market Master Plans and Wholesale Distribution Center Development Strategy.* Consultant's report. Manila.

5.2 Uzbekistan

Horticulture value chains in Uzbekistan lack marketing capacity and transportation infrastructure, show weak linkages between value chain actors, and lack modern storage and processing capacity. These weaknesses are reflected in postharvest losses, which are estimated to be up to 30%. A Horticulture Value Chain Infrastructure Project for Uzbekistan aims to finance wholesale market and logistics centers designed to access export markets and reduce postharvest losses through improved infrastructure and cold chain practices.[19] ADB has previously provided assistance to the sector through the Horticulture Value Chain Development Project that supports enhancing agricultural productivity and the sustainable financial and economic viability of horticulture producers and agribusiness enterprises.[20]

ADB's Horticulture Value Chain Infrastructure Project designs agricultural logistics centers, which serve several value chain functions (sales, storage, processing, certification, customs clearance, and support services) in a single location. This will facilitate the smooth flow of produce from producer to consumer through investment in modern product handling technologies and professional center management. The project will help many horticulture farmers and entrepreneurs boost their investments; maintain and expand employment; and provide stable incomes for themselves, their employees, and suppliers.

5.3 Pakistan

An ADB-financed assessment of horticulture value chains linking the Lahore wholesale market identified inefficiencies that result in several negative impacts, including the low share of farmers in consumer prices, high price volatility, and postharvest losses.[21] Producers' share in retail prices ranges from 15% to 20%. Due to mishandling of perishable products, poor transportation, and inadequate storage facilities and market infrastructure, postharvest losses account for about 30%–40% of total production. ADB's assessment concluded that existing wholesale markets need to be relocated to the outskirts of Lahore, while retail activities in their current locations will be maintained. A new wholesale market that can offer additional services (such as phytosanitary inspections, certifications, traceability, laboratory examination, e-auction, banking, catering and restaurants, accommodation, and price information) is recommended.

---

[19]   ADB. 2018. *Report and Recommendation of the President to the Board of Directors: Proposed Loan to the Republic of Uzbekistan for the Horticulture Value Chain Infrastructure Project.* Manila.

[20]   ADB. 2018. *Report and Recommendation of the President to the Board of Directors: Proposed Loan for Additional Financing to the Republic of Uzbekistan for the Horticulture Value Chain Infrastructure Project.* Manila.

[21]   ADB. 2019. *Dysfunctional Horticulture Value Chains and the Need for Modern Marketing Infrastructure: The Case of Pakistan.* Papers and Briefs. Manila.

6 RECOMMENDED APPROACH FOR PUBLIC SECTOR PROJECTS TO INCREASE FARMING INCOMES

6.1 Approach to Public Sector Projects

The improvements identified in this paper will increase farm incomes, but will require an integrated approach, including

    (i)   public investment in assets (farm stalls and wholesale center);
    (ii)   financing of private assets (alternative crops, processing, and potentially retail chain model packaging for farmer and group brands);
    (iii) support services (training and governance support); and
    (iv) regulatory review (competition arrangements).

These activities should be carried out under the proposed ADB Loan Program.

6.2 Approach to Private Sector Engagement

The improvements identified herein will require engagement with farmers through CGGs and other supply chain participants. Engagement with processors will be primarily through financing activities for processing assets. Engagement with wholesalers will be through development of the wholesale center. Engagement with retailers would be the responsibility of the CGGs on a commercial basis. In all cases, engagement may be mediated by whatever institutional recommendations that would emerge from the review of competition arrangements. For example, there may be a consultative forum involving stakeholders along the value chain to consider a code of conduct or standard form contracts.

6.3 Recommendations

- The statistical base for vegetables needs to be enhanced to cover production of vegetables currently in demand, such as green leafy vegetables, on a basis consistent with the statistics already available for imports of these products. There is also a lack of data on vegetable prices along the supply chain, which needs to be addressed.

- Development of farm stalls, where vegetable producers (especially small-sized household producers) can eliminate intermediary costs and sell directly to consumers, should be pilot tested at selected points in Ulaanbaatar and in relatively high-traffic rural locations (e.g., auto and railroad crossings). The pilot testing should assess the economic cost–benefit for farmers of selling via this value chain.

- The value chain entailing direct supply of vegetables from farmers to processors can eliminate intermediary costs and potentially increase farmer returns. Increased processing of vegetables would encourage more use of this value chain and should be facilitated through support for additional large-scale processing investments, such as those currently supported through ADB's Agriculture and Rural Development Project. These could be located in production supply areas within target *soums*, if economically feasible, or in Ulaanbaatar. Processors should be encouraged to implement supply contracts with CGGs in the target *soums*.

- The value chain entailing direct supply of vegetables by farmers to retailers can eliminate intermediary costs and potentially increase farmer returns. Retailers should be encouraged to enter into strategic partnerships with CGGs to support year-round supply of produce that meets retailer standards.

- CGGs should develop group brands, especially for high-value vegetables, in close collaboration with retailers, including through co-branding.

- CGGs should evaluate, with their retail partners, the development of group packaging and labeling of produce that meets consumer needs.

- Where economically justified and supported by strategic marketing relationships, support should be given to CGGs' purchase of packaging and labeling facilities.

- Increase in supply on a year-round basis should be facilitated by expanding greenhouses, especially winter greenhouses. This could be supported on a similar basis to ADB's Agriculture and Rural Development Project approach on enabling expansion of processing facilities.

- In expanding greenhouse production, particular attention needs to be given to training farmers in production technology through CGGs and learning from the experience of successful greenhouse producers.

- The development of an appropriately located new wholesale selling center in Ulaanbaatar should be investigated. Such a center would address several current shortcomings in the value chain for wholesale supply of vegetables. It would (i) replace the current outdated and unsustainably located wholesale marketplace; (ii) provide CGGs with access to a central wholesale outlet with storage facilities, which maximizes competition; and (iii) enable collection and dissemination of data on prices, which can facilitate price transparency and form part of a modern integrated logistical system.

- The adequacy of the current competition regulations relating to farm produce supply should be reviewed, including examination of the potential for introduction of codes of conduct and standard form contracts for the sale of produce by farmers. This will strengthen the bargaining power of farmers in their direct dealings with processors and retailers.

- Production of seeds in Mongolia tailored to Mongolian conditions should be expanded, through the provision of additional infrastructure for seed multiplication by research institutes, in collaboration with private seed companies.

■ Mongolia needs to align its food safety guidelines and provide more public health advocacy for suggested vegetable intake per person. The absence of reliable quality assurance testing of farm inputs, such as pesticides, increases production costs and poses a potential risk for environmental pollution. The lack of agrochemical residue testing capacity at government agencies threatens food safety and access to premium price marketing opportunities. In 2017, the annual per capita consumption rates were about 111.3 g/day of potatoes and 142.4 g/day of vegetables, which are less than the 120 g/day of potatoes and 260 g/day of vegetables recommended by the Ministry of Health in Decree No. A/74, 2017.

APPENDIX: CASE STUDY

The Greenhouse Vegetable Growers Federation members produce green vegetables in their winter greenhouses when the outside temperature is below 0°C. (photos by Altanbadralt Sharkhuu).

Household greenhouse vegetable growers who are members of the Greenhouse Vegetable Growers Federation have greenhouses right in their backyard. (photos by Altanbadralt Sharkhuu).